ID0770707

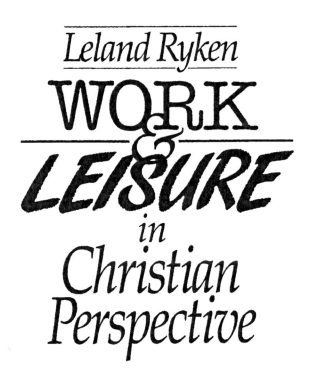

Leland Ryken

WORK & LEISURE

in Christian Perspective

Wipf and Stock Publishers

EUGENE, OREGON

Wipf and Stock Publishers
199 West 8th Avenue, Suite 3
Eugene, Oregon 97401

Work & Leisure in Christian Perspective
By Ryken, Leland
Copyright©1987 Ryken, Leland
ISBN: 1-57910-959-4
Publication date: May, 2002
Previously published by Multnomah Press, 1987.

For Margaret

Contents

Preface

The most disconcerting feature of working on this book was the reaction of my friends when I told them that my latest writing project was a book on work and leisure. The customary response was uproarious laughter. I infer that I was judged to have intimate knowledge of work but rather limited acquaintance with leisure.

As I was charging forward toward completion of the book, I had leisure (loosely defined) forced upon me. It began with the eerie sound of a ladder sliding on the driveway. It proceeded to the clanging sound, heard throughout the neighborhood, of the ladder hitting the driveway. The aftermath was two broken arms and a broken nose.

The experience gave me personal insights into what I had written during the preceding weeks. There were lessons about how God has ordained times of rest from work, about the need at a certain point to let go of striving, and about the benefits of time protected from the inroads of work.

As my time of inactivity wore on, I learned even more about work than about leisure. I learned that work is indeed a gift from God. To be unable to work is abnormal and debilitating to one's well-being. I recall how I longed to be able to do even such despised work as taking out the garbage and cutting back the trumpet vines (which had occasioned the accident with the ladder).

Work and leisure are God's gifts to the human race. Attitudes toward them in our society are dominated by a secular outlook. Thinking Christianly about work and leisure should be a priority for the church.

Introduction

Work and Leisure: A Critical Issue

Work and leisure are a major concern for both Christians and society at large. We feel guilty about our work, and we feel guilty about our leisure. We do not understand either of them very well.

Contemporary Attitudes

Our society entertains contradictory attitudes toward work. Workaholics have turned work into their religion. One writer found that they spend nearly half their time—seventy hours per week or more—working at their job. But two of my acquaintances who have sat next to business executives on plane trips tell a different story. Employers generally think the work ethic is either dead or dying. The head of a business with branches throughout the country said his company tries to hire workers only from the Midwest because they tend to have better attitudes toward work.

As a society, we betray our impoverished work ethic by our slogans. On a recent car trip I was passed by a truck with the following jingle painted on the back: "I owe, I owe, so off to work I go." Here, in rather crude form, is a dominant work ethic today. It views work in mercenary terms—the thing that makes our acquisitive lifestyle possible.

Or consider the sign I saw on an office door: "I'd rather be fishing." Here is another prevalent attitude toward work: it is a necessary evil. Leisure is what we value, and work is something we put up with as a means to that end.

We signal our uneasiness about our attitudes toward work by our quips:

"Work fascinates me—I can sit and watch it for hours."
"Thank God it's Friday."
"Hard work may not kill me, but why take a chance?"
"I'm not lazy—I just don't like to work."

I recently saw a license plate frame that said, "Retired—no more worry, no more hurry, no more boss."

Work is a problem for all of us. We do not go around saying, "Thank God it's Monday." When we overwork we feel guilty about the way work robs us of time for other areas of life, including family activities and devotional exercises. At other times we feel guilty for disliking our work. Who does not resonate with Thoreau's comment that the laboring person "has not leisure for a true integrity day by day. He has no time to be anything but a machine."[1]

The Church and Work

The church should be proclaiming a clear message on a subject of such universal concern. It once did. For the original Protestants and Puritans, work was a favorite sermon topic, as surviving sermons show. But when did you last hear (or preach) a sermon on work?

The church is responsible to relate Christian doctrine to all of life in terms lay people can understand. There was a time when it did so with regard to work. What has happened since then can be summed up in a phrase used by W. R. Forrester in his book *Christian Vocation*—the "lost provinces of religion."[2] As I contend throughout this book, it is time to enlarge the province of Christianity so it again influences the public forum on the topics of work and leisure.

I doubt that attitudes toward work are very different in our churches than in our culture at large. We find the normal quota of workaholics in the pew on Sunday morning. And what percentage of Christians view their work with the sense of calling that the Reformers proclaimed with such clarity?

The lack of a Christian work ethic is particularly acute among young people. A recent book-length study surveyed attitudes among young people enrolled at Christian colleges and seminaries. One of the conclusions drawn by the researcher who wrote the book was this:

> What has been seen thus far merely confirms what
> is already well known about the place and value of
> work for Evangelicalism—that work has lost any
> spiritual and eternal significance and that it is impor-
> tant only insofar as it fosters certain qualities of the
> personality.[3]

The Church and Leisure

As for leisure, the church has never been able to make up its mind about it. The Bible says little about leisure directly. Christians through the centuries have also said and thought little about it, preferring to feel guilty about time spent in leisure. As the title of a book on the subject suggests, when Christians relax they feel guilty.

The church has often opted for easy answers to the question of leisure. One of these answers has been to reject leisure as bad. In the Catholic Middle Ages, church leaders such as Augustine and Tertullian advised Christians to stay away from cultural amusements such as plays and festivals and stick in- stead to the spiritual life. The distrust of "worldly amusements" has also run strong in Protestantism in every era of its history.

At the other extreme is the practice of ignoring the ques- tion of leisure. The resulting problem is that whenever the church has refused to think about the question of culture it has usually ended up imitating the practices of a secular society. This has been a common trend in our century. Christians adopt cultural practices just as they are going out of vogue in the secular world. By being a step behind the world at large, we feel safe in following the lead of a secular culture. What we casually watch on television today would have shocked Christians twenty years ago. Robert K. Johnston correctly observes that

> it is surprising that . . . the Christian Church has put so little thought into the person at play. Rather than ground their discussion in biblical reflection and careful observation of play itself, Christians have most often been content to allow Western culture to shape their understanding of the human at play.[4]

The church needs to grapple with the question of leisure more seriously than it does. The New England Puritan Cotton Mather preached a sermon to his congregation about the uses of leisure during the winter months. But when did you last hear (or preach) a sermon on leisure?

Of course it is a difficult and touchy issue to analyze and criticize leisure pursuits in which people are already engaged. Perhaps pastors feel intimidated by the prospect. As a writer, I have felt free from those constraints.

Distinctives of This Book

This book fills several gaps that I quickly noted as I did the research for the book. Most of the writing on work and leisure is from a secular perspective. While it delineates the contemporary issues to which the Christian faith speaks, it offers almost no help in thinking Christianly about work and leisure.

Of course these writers do not hesitate to make slurring remarks about the role of religion in the history of work and leisure. "The Protestant ethic" has long been the favorite whipping post. A leading purpose of a Christian analysis of work and leisure is to set the record straight about the common charges made against Christianity, especially the original Protestants. I have attempted to do so in this book.

Books written by Christians on work and leisure also leave a lot to be desired. They too tend to perpetuate the inaccurate stereotype about the Puritans. The authors are often strangers to what is best in their own tradition.

Nor has the question of what constitutes the authoritative source for our thinking about work and leisure been answered very satisfactorily in the existing literature. I have read a lot that purports to be "a theology of" work or leisure that is no more than an author's private thinking on the subject. Some "theologies" of play are particularly frivolous. Sometimes the claim to be a "theology" of play struck me as a straight-faced joke being played on a gullible public.

I have written from the presupposition that the Bible is the final authority of truth on the issues about which it speaks. Of course it is important to adduce the biblical data that is actually relevant to the subject of work and leisure. I have read books and articles that bombarded me with biblical verses but that left me wondering what those verses could possibly have to do with work or leisure.

One thing that sets this book apart from most other books on the subject is that it *combines* the subjects of work and leisure. There are lots of books on work and many on leisure. But it is self-defeating to keep these in separate compartments. Work and leisure together make up a whole. They influence each other, partly because they compete with each other for our time. They derive much of their meaning from each other. I have therefore discussed them together.

The logic underlying this book is one of integration. In the first four chapters I assemble the data on work and leisure that any good discussion of these subjects should consider. These chapters are the agenda of issues to which the Christian faith speaks.

In the last four chapters and the conclusion I have set up a dialogue between these issues and the Christian faith. I would urge my readers not to expect something from the early chapters that they are not designed to give. Nor should they be impatient with these chapters. If Christianity is the answer, we first have to understand the questions.

As my last comment implies, this book is also written on a principle of problem and solution. I conclude on the basis of evidence from research that work and leisure constitute problems in contemporary society. I have analyzed the nature of the problems and explored how a Christian view of work and leisure answers those problems.

I have written about work and leisure at the level of general principles. I will leave it to my readers to apply what I say to their own lives. It should not be hard to do so. After all, work and leisure make up our daily lives.

Introduction, Notes

1. Henry David Thoreau, as quoted by Tim Hansel, *When I Relax I Feel Guilty* (Elgin, Ill.: David C. Cook Publishing Co., 1979), 34.

2. W. R. Forrester, *Christian Vocation* (New York: Charles Scribners Sons, 1953), 169.

3. James Davison Hunter, *Evangelicalism: The Coming Generation* (Chicago: University of Chicago Press, 1987), 56.

4. Robert K. Johnston, *The Christian at Play* (Grand Rapids, Mich.: Wm. B. Eerdmans Publishing Co., 1983), 83.

PART 1

ISSUES IN WORK AND LEISURE

Chapter 1

Understanding Work and Leisure

Work and leisure are the central ingredients of our daily living. They take up most of our time. Yet we are so busy doing them that we do not take the time to understand them. Christians collect proof texts on work and leisure from the Bible without first inquiring into their inherent nature.

The purpose of this chapter is to construct an anatomy of work and leisure. I will analyze their nature, functions, and rewards, as well as supplying some basic definitions.

TIME: WHAT WORK AND LEISURE SHARE

The subject of time is a good starting point for understanding the interrelated phenomena of work and leisure. Time is the arena within which work and leisure struggle for our attention, along with a few other basic human activities, during the course of a typical day.

Obligatory and Discretionary Activities

The simplest dichotomy into which we can divide the twenty-four hours that make up the day is between activities that are obligatory and those that are discretionary—between activities we have to do and those we choose to do. These should be viewed as two poles on a continuum, not as two separate columns of activities.

On the obligatory end of the spectrum we find those daily activities that are required to sustain life. They include personal care (sleeping, eating, clothing), housework (preparing meals, cleaning the house, cutting the lawn), the job that produces one's income, task-related studying, and social obligations (helping a spouse or roommate, overseeing a child's homework, helping a friend move). While work does not comprise all that exists on the obligatory end of the scale, it belongs with other activities that cluster together in the realm of obligations.

At the discretionary end of the spectrum we find those activities that are usually placed into the category of leisure— entertainment, sports, recreation, hobbies, and other free time activities. These are things that we do because we want to, and that we do for their own sake.

Semileisure Activities

As we ponder the scale, it becomes evident that some activities fall into a middle category. They are either a mixture of obligation and freedom, or they fall into one category or the other depending on the person or occasion. Examples include gardening, decorating a room, or serving on a committee. Traveling to work or some other required activity is work for some people and recreation for others. So are physical exercise, building bookshelves, or refinishing a piece of furniture.

Then too we all have obligations that do not fall into the category of work, though their obligatory nature at the same time removes them from the realm of leisure. Attending Little League practices, reading a book in order to keep informed, caring for pets, and optional shopping are examples.

It is small wonder, therefore, that authorities on the subject have coined the term *semileisure* to cover activities that do not fall clearly into the category of either work or leisure. One of them explains, "Here is an activity part practical, part nonpractical, so to speak, in varying proportions."[1] Activities that fall into this category often stem from relationships. It is also common for these activities to begin as freely chosen and gradually assume the quality of a duty. One thinks, for example, of doing extra work for pay and of various types of volunteer work.

In sum, we can picture our daily activities as falling somewhere on the following scale:

Obligation	Semileisure	Freedom
(work)		(leisure)

The scale I have just outlined will be important throughout this book. It shows at a glance how interrelated work and leisure are. They are not separate elements of our lives but rather complementary aspects of a single whole. To talk about leisure without considering the constraints of the obligatory activities in our daily routine is unrealistic. We can increase one segment of the continuum only by subtracting something else.

It is also apparent that necessary work takes precedence over leisure in our daily routine. Leisure is something we can engage in only after our basic physical necessities are satisfied. To define leisure as nonwork is not, as we shall see, an adequate definition, but the scale shows at a glance that freedom from obligation or necessity is at least a prerequisite for leisure.

Equally important is the recognition of a category of semileisure activities. For many activities in life, it is up to us whether they will be experienced as work or leisure. To move work toward the right side of the scale and to enlarge the sphere in which we feel the spirit of freedom and choice is a laudable goal. Christianity does not endorse masochism or gloom. Even leisure in work becomes possible if we approach work in the right spirit. A main theme of this book is the desirability of enlarging the freedom side of the ledger.

Finally, the scale I have discussed has a special relevance to Christian activities. Many spiritual and moral acts that Christians perform have a combined sense of duty and pleasure. Christians pray, attend Bible studies and worship services, serve on committees of Christian organizations, and volunteer their time to help people in need, partly because they regard these as obligations of the Christian life, and partly because they want to do them. The whole area of "Christian ministry" occupies a huge part of the middle of the scale for many Christians, though secular sources ignore that fact.

THE NATURE OF WORK

To understand work, we need to distinguish between *job* and *work*. Work for which we are paid or by which we earn our livelihood goes by the common name of *job* or *labor*. But this is only part of the work that we do. Discussions that limit work to one's job end up being much less helpful than they seem to promise. We need, of course, to develop a Christian perspective on labor, but to stop there is to leave some of the most problematic areas of our daily lives untouched. We also need to make sense of vacuuming the house, taking out the garbage, and driving children to music lessons. The problem of work is often most acute in these areas because getting paid for labor at once lends a kind of sanction to it that is lacking in other work.

Work, then, includes our job, but it extends well beyond it. It includes all that we are obliged to do to meet our physical and social needs. With this basic definition in place, let's look at some complementary ways by which we understand the nature or meaning of work. We will basically be exploring the answers that people give when they are asked, "Why do you work?"

Work as a Means of Providing for Life's Needs and Wants

At the most elemental level, work is a means of providing for the needs and desires of life. As such, it is basically utilitarian. Whatever else work may add to life, it supplies the money by which we acquire goods and services, or it simply makes life around the house possible. To live our lives, we need to cook meals and take the car to the gas station and shovel the snow from the driveway.

Of course this acquisitive view of work that links it to consumption extends to more than satisfying the necessities of life. It also becomes the means toward supplying the products and activities that make up a total lifestyle. It is apparent, then, how drastically work becomes affected by the consumer society in which we live, given further impetus by the expectation of upward social mobility.

Such a view of work is on a collision course with certain basic Christian assumptions, as we will see later in this book. If not balanced by other attitudes, the view of work as a source of income robs work of intrinsic value and of other ends besides personal advancement and consumption, and it quickly produces the workaholic syndrome.

Work as a Curse

Regarding work as a necessity because it supplies the basic needs and wants of life does not have to turn it into a curse, but in fact it often does so because it accentuates the obligatory nature of work. We tend to find burdensome anything to which we are driven by necessity. This link is suggested by the biblical account of how work became a curse after the Fall:

> cursed is the ground because of you;
> in toil you shall eat of it all the days of your life.
> . . . .
> In the sweat of your face
> you shall eat bread.
> (Genesis 3:17, 19)

Here we see the curse of work put into a context of earning one's daily sustenance.

The element of curse in work is intrinsic to life in a fallen world. Evidence of the nature and extent to which work is a curse is readily available from sociological and psychological sources and will emerge in the next chapter, where I discuss the problem of work in our own society. The curse of work cannot be ignored, though we can partly redeem work from its curse. Any naive glorification of work is refuted by a long, hard look around us, as well as by some introspection into our own feelings toward what we do in a typical day. Nor does the Christian faith take a naively optimistic attitude toward work. Taking out the garbage and cleaning the bathroom are nothing less than unpleasant in themselves.

Work as a Means of Production

Work can also be viewed from an economic perspective. Viewed thus, it is obviously a means of production. It is measured in terms of its value to the employer or the laborer.

Given this economic context, labor becomes something that an employer "buys" and that a worker "sells." Both work and worker become something that are "worth" this or that amount. Labor becomes another commodity on the market.

Of course this dimension of work carries inherent opportunities for perverted attitudes toward work. Work can become as impersonal as the machinery in a factory. It is sold and bought at the market rate, with the result that some workers naturally view their work as worth less than that of others. Instead of being viewed as a calling with inherent worth, work often becomes mercenary, a means to financial ends. The laborer's identity becomes linked to the size of his or her paycheck. And the question, "What good does this work accomplish?" is replaced by the question, "How much does it pay?" Here, in fact, is one of the problems about work that the Christian faith must address.

Work as Human Achievement

Thus far I have viewed work in terms of its extrinsic motivations and rewards. But a more idealized view is also possible. Some types of work carry their own reward because we regard them in terms of personal accomplishment. The sense of achievement can include either the product resulting from the work or the activity of doing the work itself. The attitude of accomplishment, moreover, often extends to work that in itself is unpleasant or even drudgery. To have completed the task is perceived as an accomplishment in itself.

There is something primordial about work. It answers a deep-seated human urge to be useful, to master something, to do something skillfully, to produce something tangible. Karl Marx put it this way:

> Labor is the very touchstone for man's self-realization, the medium of creating the world of his desire. . . . Man . . . labors to transform his world, to put his own mark on it, to make it his, and to make himself at home in it.[2]

Of course this view of work as achievement can lead to either a humanistic view of human greatness or a Christian stance of stewardship in which ability and opportunity are accepted gratefully as God given.

Work as Psychological Satisfaction

Work can also be studied in psychological terms. Freud theorized that love and work are the two central activities by which people give meaning to life.[3]

The importance that Freud attached to work seems plausible when we consider the wide range of psychological needs that work satisfies. One is self-esteem and a sense of personal worth. This is most easily seen in the collapse in self-worth that afflicts the unemployed.[4] It also explains why a study that addressed the question, "Do the poor want to work?" found that poor people "identify their self-esteem with work as strongly as do the nonpoor."[5]

Work is also a major determinant in a person's identity. "What do you do for a living?" we ask someone we have recently met. "Do you have a job outside the home?" we ask married women. The answers to these questions quickly establish people's identity and status, both in their own eyes and those of others.

Work also serves a social function in our lives. Except for tasks done in solitude, work brings us into contact with other people. These social contacts carry either reward or frustration, but in either case they determine a great deal of what we think and feel in a given day. Retired people, moreover, often complain of the loss of social satisfaction that once accompanied work situations.

Yet another psychological need that work satisfies is the need for activity, which some psychologists regard as a basic human need. Work, whether it consists of one's job or tasks around the house, keeps us occupied. It also lends structure to the day.

Work as Service

Thus far I have viewed work in terms of self-interest, or what we get out of it. But a final ingredient in work pushes it in the direction of altruism. It is work as service to others.

Here the focus shifts outward to the effect of one's work on other individuals and on society as a whole. This, in fact, is one of the rewards of work: it benefits others as well as oneself. We acknowledge this ideal whenever we pay tribute to a person for what he or she has done for humanity.

Of course this ideal is more easily discerned in service-oriented jobs or volunteer work that serves the public. Correspondingly, one of the problems of work on the assembly line where one does not see the results of one's work is that the sense of service tends to evaporate.

Summary

Understanding work requires that we think about it in at least six dimensions. Work provides for life's needs and wants and is a means of economic production. It carries with it a constant possibility of being a curse or drudgery, but positively it has the potential to supply a sense of human achievement, psychological satisfaction, and service to humanity.

These are the points at which work intersects with the Christian faith. It is not my purpose at this early stage in the book to show how the Christian faith speaks to these facets of work. Instead, these form an agenda of issues that will recur throughout the pages that follow.

THE ETHICS OF WORK

Another general framework within which work must be understood is its ethical dimensions. Here too I will eventually relate the principles to a specifically Christian framework, but for the moment I am interested in the more general ethical terms that apply to work.

The very phrase *work ethic* suggests one such category. It is no doubt true that there are many specific work ethics, but when we use the term in the singular we acknowledge a generic moral outlook that values work and regards it as something good.

A work ethic implies several related things. It assumes that the *active life* and not simply the contemplative life is worthy. It implies that *industriousness* and a degree of *self-reliance* are private and public virtues. In addition, a work ethic usually implies a *social concern* for the health of society, and this is usually tinged with a feeling of *patriotism*.

There is no standard term by which to name the ethical viewpoint that stands opposed to the work ethic. But there are clearly individuals and societies that lack a work ethic. They are characterized by a high degree of idleness, low economic achievement, lack of pride in one's work, low regard for the quality of one's work, tolerance of laziness, and a parasitic reliance on others to sustain life.

Another ethical outlook that fosters work is *utilitarianism*. After all, work achieves practical results that are useful to individuals, families, and societies. Conversely, people and societies that have little feeling for what is useful produce an anemic work ethic.

It is apparent that work can flourish within ethical systems that espouse two opposed attitudes. One of these is an affirmation of *self-fulfillment*. To work is to satisfy certain innate personal needs. An ethical outlook that belittles the individual's self-realization usually ends up with an impoverished work ethic. In fact, many jobs in a technological society exist only when we disregard the worker's self-fulfillment.

The opposing ethical viewpoint that might still find a place for work is an ethic of *self-sacrifice* or *self-denial*. Given the element of drudgery in work, work would remain an option if one believed that self-denial is inherently virtuous. While this can be given a specifically Christian application, other ethical outlooks have also honored work within a context of self-sacrifice.

A final ethical stance important to the subject of work is *servanthood* or *service to the common good*. Work can thrive within an atmosphere governed solely by self-interest, but it rarely does so. Not only does a devotion to the welfare of the state or community often buttress motives of self-interest, it can even sustain work that people do not find personally beneficial.

In sum, work derives its sanction from a range of ethical premises, including the beliefs that work is inherently virtuous, useful, self-fulfilling, self-denying, or a service to humanity. All of these can be placed in a context of Christian ethics, and once we do so, other ethical considerations such as stewardship and calling also come into play, as we will see in a later chapter.

Defining Leisure

Defining work is relatively simple. By contrast, definitions of leisure multiply indefinitely. In the next several pages we will explore the range of definitions, noting especially the three main categories of definition, which relate leisure to time, activity, and a state of soul or mind. Let me say at the outset that no one of these definitions is by itself complete, but together they establish the issues that are relevant to an understanding of leisure.

Leisure as Free Time

Time provides a good starting point for understanding leisure. Earlier I noted that we live our daily lives on a time scale. At one end of the continuum is necessary or obligatory work. It comprises the activities that sustain life. At the other end of the time scale we find discretionary activities. This is what we ordinarily call leisure. In the middle are activities we can call semileisure.

One ingredient of leisure is that it is *nonwork*. Work is done under a sense of duty or obligation. I do not thereby prejudge the question of whether some work might not have the quality of leisure. But to define leisure in the first place requires that we begin by contrasting it to work and other necessities. One authority notes,

> Contemporary leisure is defined by contrast not just to one's job, but to all of the ordinary necessities and obligations of existence, and it must be remembered that they who have and use leisure regard it as part of the dialectic of daily living.[6]

Even the etymology of the word suggests that leisure means free time. The word and concept have been traced back to two roots. One is the the Old French word *leisir*, from the Latin *licere*, meaning "to be allowed or to be lawful." Our word *license* comes from the same root. The key concept is freedom to do something.

If we ask what we are free *from* in leisure, it is obvious that we are free from the constraints of necessity or obligation. Leisure in this sense is freedom to do what we want to do in a relatively unforced manner.

The other root word to which leisure has been traced points in the same direction. It is the Greek word *skole* or the Latin *schola*, from which we derive our word *school*. At its origin, the word carried the idea "to halt or cease," later acquiring the connotation of having time to spare for oneself and one's development as a person.[7]

The idea of leisure as time in which we are free to choose our own activities underlies some often quoted definitions of leisure by modern authorities, including the following:

> Leisure is activity chosen in relative freedom for its qualities of satisfaction.[8]
>
> Leisure is activity apart from the obligations of work, family, and society to which the individual turns at will, for either relaxation, diversion, or broadening his knowledge. . . .[9]
>
> Leisure is time beyond that which is required for existence . . . and subsistence. . . . It is discretionary time, the time to be used according to our own judgement or choice.[10]
>
> Leisure is time free from work and other obligations and it also encompasses activities which are characterised by a feeling of (comparative) freedom.[11]

All of these definitions agree that leisure is a contrast to work and other obligations, and that it is freely chosen instead of being done under obligation. Of course an activity must *feel* like leisure and must be *perceived* as freely chosen to rank as leisure. Cutting the lawn or attending a party is either work or leisure, depending on how a person perceives it in terms of obligation or discretion.

An important part of leisure—and part of its function in human experience—lies in its status as an escape. By itself it has little meaning and quickly palls. Placed as a complement to work, it assumes meaning. Someone has called leisure "a parenthesis in life."[12]

Although leisure is not synonymous with play, these two have much in common, and Johan Huizinga's famous description of play will help fill out what I am saying about leisure as enlightened escape.[13] Play, claims Huizinga, is a voluntary activity. It is superfluous, beyond the ordinary necessity of life. It is disinterested, standing "outside the immediate satisfaction of wants and appetites." It "adorns" and "amplifies" life. Being different from ordinary life, play is limited in its time and space, and it is governed by its own rules. In sum, play is

a free activity standing quite consciously outside "ordinary" life. . . . It is an activity connected with no material interest, and no profit can be gained by it. It proceeds within its own proper boundaries of time and space according to fixed rules and in an orderly manner. It promotes the formation of social groupings. . . .

All of this is true of leisure in general as well as play.

Leisure as Activity

To define leisure as nonworking time in which people are free to choose their activities is a necessary but insufficient definition. Having cleared a space for leisure, as it were, we need to put some positive ingredients into that space. For this reason it has seemed natural to think of leisure as the pursuit of certain activities.

Cultural pursuits, for example, have traditionally been classified as leisure. Reading a book, attending a concert or play, visiting an art gallery or museum, and listening to music are leisure activities.

Recreation is a second main category of leisure activities. Such recreation runs the gamut from sports to vacationing, from playing a table game to skiing.

The broad category of *entertainment* ranks as a third major leisure activity in the modern world, with the mass media topping the list. Watching television, going to see a movie, listening to the radio or cassette player, and reading magazines have absorbed a larger and larger share of the leisure scene in the later twentieth century. By 1983, for example, average daily household watching of television had risen to more than seven hours.[14]

Hobbies and crafts also belong to the list of activities the world puts into the category of leisure. Collecting things from stamps to antiques rates as a hobby. So does restoring things (furniture, cars) and making things (model train layouts, picture frames). Photography, gardening, and many types of puttering around the house can likewise rise to the level of leisure.

Finally, many *social activities* fall into the sphere of leisure. Visiting with friends or relatives, informal conversations in the hallway, going on a family picnic, or attending a church potluck dinner are obvious examples.

I have taken the time to categorize leisure activities because doing so highlights an important fact: our leisure activities exceed the leisure time we usually feel we have at our disposal. When asked in the abstract how much leisure they have, busy people think in terms of leisure *time* and conclude that they have little leisure in their lives. The range of activities that make up leisure helps to modify that assessment at least a little.

The list of leisure activities also suggests something of the range of pursuits I intend this book to cover. My approach to the subject is at the level of underlying principles, but I expect that we will apply the principles to our own specific leisure pursuits.

It is also important to note that defining leisure as time spent in specific activities is incomplete by itself. To rate as leisure, an activity must include the elements of freedom and choice that I noted earlier. The attitude accompanying a given activity determines whether it is work or leisure.

For some people, jogging is leisure. For others, it is work—an activity governed by the utilitarian end of physical fitness and having the quality of drudgery. Golf is leisure for people doing it in their free time but work for those who do it to cultivate a business relationship. Having someone over for dinner can be either a social duty or a leisure activity. Work done as "moonlighting" can be just another job designed to produce extra income, but it can also meet all the criteria of leisure.

A final significance of defining leisure in terms of activity is that it shows leisure to be the opposite not only of necessary work (as noted in the definition of leisure as time) but also of idleness. Leisure is not synonymous with free time, though free time is usually a prerequisite for it. Leisure is time devoted to freely chosen activities that are inherently pleasurable and satisfying. Many of these activities require effort and are even physically or mentally strenuous, but they are experienced as leisure because they are freely chosen and carry the rewards of leisure.

Leisure as a Quality of Life

Following the usual procedure, I have thus far defined leisure in terms of time (nonworking time in which people are free to do what they choose) and in terms of activity. But the concept of leisure reaches its fullest dignity when we narrow the range still further and define it in terms of a quality that it bestows on life. One of the standard sources on the subject, Sebastian de Grazia's book *Of Time, Work, and Leisure*, asserts that

> leisure and free time live in two different worlds. We have got in the habit of thinking them the same. Anybody can have free time. Not everybody can have leisure. . . . Leisure refers to a state of being, a condition of man, which few desire and fewer achieve. [15]

What things, then, make up the attitude that merits the designation *leisure*? As a beginning, we can agree with someone who writes that "leisure is a matter of the individual's perception rather than of rigid time-based or activity-based definitions. It is rooted in enjoyment and reflects degrees of pleasure and satisfaction." [16] In other words, leisure is a state of feeling satisfied—a kind of luxurious well-being.

The most vigorous attempt to define leisure as a positive quality of life has been made from a Catholic perspective by Josef Pieper. [17] "Leisure'" writes Pieper, "is a mental and spiritual attitude—it is not simply the result of external factors, it is not the inevitable result of spare time, a holiday, a week-end or a vacation. It is, in the first place, an attitude of mind, a condition of the soul."

According to Pieper, several ingredients help to produce this condition of the soul. One is "an attitude of non-activity, of inward calm, of . . . letting things happen." It is "a receptive attitude of mind" and one that eludes "those who grab and grab hold." Also important is a sense of celebration conceived as joy in the acceptance of one's place in the world. In leisure, moreover, "the truly human values are saved and preserved."

This is obviously a high ideal for leisure. It asserts that leisure is more than doing; it is also being. While I do not wish to exclude free time activities that fall short of this ideal, a main goal of this book is to encourage us all to upgrade the quality of our leisure pursuits. There is a terrible tendency to drift into mediocrity in our leisure life by default instead of actively choosing the excellent. When we define leisure in terms of human enrichment, it again emerges as the opposite, not only of work, but of idleness.

Summary

We have seen that definitions of leisure include three complementary aspects. Leisure begins as time free from constraints of obligation or necessity. Beyond that, it consists of certain activities that are conventionally classified as leisure. In their highest forms these activities add important qualities to human life, including satisfaction, enrichment, receptivity, and celebration.

THE REWARDS AND FUNCTIONS OF LEISURE

Defining leisure is one way to understand it. Equally helpful is identifying the rewards and goals that people attach to leisure, since these too help us understand what it is and what it is designed to accomplish.

Leisure, for example, serves the purpose of balancing or compensating for the strain of work and obligation. As such it is part of the rhythm of life. While it would belittle leisure to see it only in its relationship to work, it is necessary to see it partly in the context of what one authority calls "the search for repose."[18]

There are, of course, other rewards to leisure. Dumazedier identifies three primary functions of leisure: relaxation, entertainment, and personal development.[19] Relaxation "provides recovery from fatigue" and "repairs the physical and nervous damage wrought by the tensions of daily pressures." This is "the recuperative function of leisure." Entertainment, in turn, "spells deliverance from boredom." As for personal development, leisure "permits a broader, readier social participation on the one hand and on the other, a willing cultivation of the physical and mental self over and above utilitarian considerations of job or practical advancement."

Someone else has approached the subject by identifying the ideals that leisure at its best can meet. The list includes pleasure, learning, playfulness, celebration, and self-actualization.[20] Writing from a Christian perspective, Robert Lee paints a similar picture:

> Leisure is the growing time of the human spirit. Leisure provides the occasion for learning and freedom, for growth and expression, for rest and restoration, for rediscovering life in its entirety.[21]

Earlier in this chapter I noted that one of the psychological and social functions of work is that it helps to establish a person's identity. The same is potentially true for leisure, though our overvaluing of work and undervaluing of leisure tend to obscure this. There is no logical reason why my friend at church should be more identified as an investment banker at work than as an expert harpsichord player in his leisure time. In fact, his education was in the area of music, and he chose work that would allow him to cultivate his avocation in music. Someone has rightly said that leisure is "the crucial life space for the expression and development of selfhood, for the working out of identities that are important to the individual."[22]

Most people would take more responsibility for the quality

of their leisure if they saw how important it can be in establishing their identity. It is partly in leisure that we discover who we are and what is expected of us. We might note in this regard that everyone has a leisure history made up of past experiences, opportunities seized or lost, satisfactions, and frustrations. Together these make up a significant part of our identity.

One authority on leisure believes that leisure is part of an innate human pursuit of what a person regards as a desirable identity.[23] To the extent people are free to make choices, they build their lives around an ideal they hold for themselves. People thus reveal "by their choices, in clothes, furniture, speech, manners, leisure activities, friends, and as far as possible work, their individual interpretation of the ideal identity they are pursuing. The goals of leisure and of life are inseparable."

Leisure is also important in establishing social relations. For one thing, many leisure activities are done with other people. Then, too, leisure pursuits at once place us into interest groups with those who enjoy the same leisure activity. Our leisure activities either enlarge or narrow the circle of people with whom we have contacts. And we choose leisure pursuits partly by how they affect the expectations of other people in our nonworking time.

This insight from leisure theory has specific application to the types of unity the church or other Christian groups have always sought to establish. Although the following statement was not made with the church in mind, I believe it has clear implications for the ideal of the church as a closely knit body:

> The social nature of much leisure would indicate
> that leisure has the special function of building community in society. In the chosen activities and relationships of leisure, the bonding of intimate groups
> such as the family and larger groups of the community takes place.[24]

To speak of the leisure function of the church may seem like trivializing the church, but in fact a large part of the spiritual and social activities of a dynamic and unified church fall within the sphere of leisure. What is needed is an upgrading of the dignity that leisure holds in the Christian world.

Of special importance is the role of leisure in family living. Leisure is one of the largest things families share—or at least ought to share. One authority comments that "the family provides the first context of leisure learning, the primary socialization about leisure values, the companions for most leisure through the life cycle, and (in the residence) the location of most leisure. . . . It is the family which usually takes the vacation trip, eats as a group, and goes to church together."[25] One study found a positive correlation between couples' satisfaction with their marriage and the proportion of time spent in shared leisure activities.[26]

Concerning the social context of leisure, it is important to note that leisure is always a learned behavior. At every stage of life, we do in our leisure time what we have learned to do. Of course this process of learning can be greatly aided by educational opportunities (broadly defined). To minimize the role of education for leisure is to settle for a rather low level of achievement through a process of inertia.

A final function of leisure is that it provides the arena within which we express personally held values. Our very choice of leisure pursuits is based on our personal values. Leisure also tests people's values or lack of them. As Robert Lee puts it,

> The problem of leisure is . . . the problem of life. . . . Leisure is a part of man's ultimate concern. It is a crucial part of the very search for meaning in life. . . . Increasingly it is in our leisure time that either the meaningfulness or the pointlessness of life will be revealed.[27]

In addition to testing our values, leisure can add to them:

> Leisure is not something added to life, a . . . diversion or . . . sigh that is often indistinguishable from

boredom. It is the process that builds meaning and purpose into life.[28]

Leisure is not peripheral to life but essential to it. One study found that people's satisfaction with life as a whole was more strongly related to satisfaction with leisure than satisfaction with their job.[29]

Summary

At its best, leisure serves many functions. It provides rest, relaxation, enjoyment, and physical and psychic health. It allows people to recover the distinctly human values, to build relationships, to strengthen family bonds, and to put themselves in touch with the world and nature. Leisure can lead to wholeness, gratitude, self-expression, self-fulfillment, creativity, personal growth, and a sense of achievement. It expands our horizons beyond the confines of the workaday world and liberates our spirits from the bondage of the everyday routine. Anything that has these potential rewards deserves more thought and understanding than it typically receives in Christian circles.

THE ETHICS OF LEISURE

Like work, leisure can be placed into a context of traditional ethical viewpoints. As we conclude this discussion of leisure, I wish to consider some of the ethical principles that apply to it, waiting until a subsequent chapter to consider the specifically Christian morality that applies to leisure.

It will be most instructive to begin by noting the outlooks to which leisure stands opposed. One of these is *idleness*. Leisure in its ideal sense is not the absence of activity or effort. It is joyous effort in activities that are self-rewarding. Leisure is the enemy of a do-nothing outlook on life. In fact, the people most deprived of leisure include the unemployed and the depressed.

A belief in the worth of leisure is also the enemy of a *utilitarian ethic* that values only activities that are directly useful to meeting one's physical needs. By its very nature, leisure is something that is nonutilitarian in the ordinary sense of mastering one's environment. There is something joyously gratuitous about leisure in that it goes beyond the requirements of life.

It is, of course, true that a utilitarian ethic sometimes finds room for leisure, but not as something inherently worthwhile in itself. People with a strong work ethic have often acknowledged the necessity and goodness of leisure but only as something that makes work possible. This is not a genuine leisure ethic.

Nor will leisure thrive when confronted with an ethic of *self-abasement*. Leisure is intrinsically pleasurable. It aims to produce delight and satisfaction. It is no wonder, therefore, that leisure always fares poorly in ethical systems that denigrate pleasure. If pleasure is wrong, leisure and play are virtually the first things to go.

Turning, then, to the positive side, the pursuit of leisure presupposes a *hedonistic ethic*, by which I mean an outlook that accepts the desirability of pleasure and enjoyment. There are, of course, Christian and non-Christian versions of what constitutes legitimate pleasure, but what I call hedonism or pleasure-seeking is the seedbed within which leisure grows, and it is not incompatible with Christianity, as a recent book by John Piper shows.[30]

A second ethical viewpoint presupposed by leisure is *humanism*. This term too has been sullied in the minds of some Christians because of its secular definitions in the twentieth century. But humanism as it has existed through the centuries has meant the striving to perfect all human possibilities in this world. It is devoted to human development and fulfillment. Such humanism can be either God-centered or man-centered.[31]

Summary

Leisure is not ethically neutral. It flourishes only when people believe in the goodness of pleasure and human fulfillment. It withers when people are lazy, preoccupied with what is useful, or given to self-denial. Perhaps we can see here the seeds of some of the negative attitudes toward leisure that have prevailed throughout the history of Christianity.

FURTHER READING

Sebastian de Grazia, *Of Time, Work, and Leisure* (1962).
Joffre Dumazedier, *Toward a Society of Leisure* (1967).
Harold D. Lehman, *In Praise of Leisure* (1974).
Geoffrey Godbey, *Leisure in Your Life: An Exploration* (1980).
John R. Kelly, *Leisure* (1982).
Stanley Parker, *Leisure and Work* (1983).

Chapter 1, Notes
_____

1. Joffre Dumazedier, *Toward a Society of Leisure*, trans. Stewart E. McClure (New York: Free Press, 1967), 18-19.

2. Quoted by Harold D. Lehman, *In Praise of Leisure* (Scottdale, Penn.: Herald Press, 1974), 82.

3. In *Civilization and Its Discontents*, Freud wrote that "the life of human beings in common . . . had a twofold foundation, i.e., the compulsion to work, created by external necessity, and the power of love." (*Great Books of the Western World*, ed. Robert M. Hutchins [Chicago: Encyclopedia Britannica, 1952] 54:782.)

4. See John C. Raines and Donna C. Day-Lower, *Modern Work and Human Meaning* (Philadelphia: Westminster Press, 1986).

5. L. Goodwin, *Do the Poor Want to Work?* (Washington, D.C.: Brookings Institution, 1972), 112.

6. Dumazedier, 14.

7. Sebastian de Grazia, *Of Time, Work, and Leisure* (New York: The Twentieth Century Fund, 1962), 12.

8. John R. Kelly, *Leisure* (Englewood Cliffs, N.J.: Prentice Hall, 1982), 7.

9. Dumazedier, 16-17.

10. Charles Brightbill, *The Challenge of Leisure* (Englewood Cliffs, N.J.: Prentice Hall, 1960), 4.

11. Stanley Parker, *The Sociology of Leisure* (New York: International Publications Service, 1976), 12.

12. Robert K. Johnston, *The Christian at Play* (Grand Rapids, Mich.: Wm. B. Eerdmans Publishing Co., 1983), 35.

13. Johan Huizinga, *Homo Ludens: A Study of the Play-Element in Culture* (1950; reprinted Boston: Beacon Press, 1955), 1-27.

14. "America: Glued to the Tube," *U. S. News and World Report*, 6 February 1984, 9.

15. de Grazia, 7-8.

16. J. Allan Patmore, *Recreation and Resources: Leisure Patterns and Leisure Places* (Oxford: Basil Blackwell, 1983), 6.

17. Josef Pieper, *Leisure the Basis of Culture*, trans. Alexander Dru (New York: Pantheon Books, 1952, 1964).

18. Dumazedier, 82.

19. Ibid., 14-16.

20. Geoffrey Godbey, *Leisure in Your Life: An Exploration* (Philadelphia: Saunders College, 1980), 289-91.

21. Robert Lee, *Religion and Leisure in America* (Nashville: Abingdon Press, 1964), 35.

22. John R. Kelly, *Leisure Identities and Interactions* (London: George Allen and Unwin, 1983), 23.

23. R. Glasser, "Leisure Policy, Identity and Work," in *Work and Leisure*, ed. J. T. Haworth and M. A. Smith (Princeton, N.J.: Princeton Book Co., 1976), 36-52.

24. Kelly, *Leisure*, 12.

25. Kelly, *Leisure*, 174. Kelly also has a helpful chapter on leisure and the family in his book *Leisure Identities and Interactions*.

26. Dennis Orthner, "Leisure Activity Patterns and Marital Satisfaction over the Marital Career," *Journal of Marriage and the Family* 37 (1975): 91-102.

27. Lee, 25-26.

28. Charles Obermeyer, "Challenges and Contradictions," in *Technology, Human Values and Leisure*, ed. Max Kaplan and Phillip Bosserman (Nashville: Abingdon Press, 1971), 222.

29. Godbey, 40.

30. John Piper, *Desiring God: Meditations of a Christian Hedonist* (Portland, Ore.: Multnomah Press, 1986).

31. For a helpful discussion of Christian humanism see Ronald B. Allen, *The Majesty of Man: The Dignity of Being Human* (Portland, Ore.: Multnomah Press, 1984).

Chapter 2

The Contemporary Crisis in Work and Leisure

*I*t would be inaccurate to say that for everyone work and leisure are in total disarray. But in the contemporary world, as observers of the social scene are well aware, work and leisure constitute major social and personal problems for many. It is my conviction that the Christian faith has good news for the problems we will uncover in this chapter, which constitutes an agenda of issues to which the Christian faith speaks.

TODAY'S WORK PROBLEM

"A job should be a job, not a death sentence."

"Jobs are demeaning. You walk out with no sense of satisfaction."

"One minute to five is the moment of triumph. You physically turn off the machine that has dictated to you all day long."

These are the statements of 3 of 133 workers interviewed by Studs Terkel for his book, *Working: People Talk about What They Do All Day and How They Feel about What They Do.*[1] Terkel's 589-page book, which has become something of a

classic on contemporary attitudes toward work, does much to
confirm that our society is suffering from a work crisis.

The opening paragraph of Terkel's introduction suggests
the extent of the crisis:

> This book, being about work, is, by its very nature,
> about violence—to the spirit as well as to the body.
> It is about ulcers as well as accidents, . . . about
> nervous breakdowns as well as kicking the dog
> around. It is, above all (or beneath all), about daily
> humiliations. To survive the day is triumph enough
> for the walking wounded among the great many of
> us.

An analysis of the dimensions of the contemporary crisis in
work reveals three major problem areas.

Too Much Work

The primary problem with work in most people's lives is
simply that there is too much of it. As noted in the previous
chapter, work extends far beyond a person's primary job and
beyond work done for pay, though the problem begins there.
A study of how Americans use their time showed that employed
men average nearly fifty-one hours per week in work for pay.[2]
This includes time spent in travel to and from work and second
jobs. Another study found an increasing minority of the male
urban labor force working fifty-five hours or more per week.[3]

The phenomenon of moonlighting is an important part of
the picture. In one survey, a third of American workers expressed a willingness to work more hours than they currently
did for more pay.[4] A 1969 study revealed that two out of five
moonlighters in the United States believed they needed to work
for extra income in order to pay for regular household expenses,
while 60 percent did it for reasons other than economic necessity.[5] An often cited case is the rubber workers in Akron, Ohio,
who worked a six-hour work day. Over half the workers took
either another full-time job or an additional part-time job.[6]

But working for pay is only part of the time we allot to work. To it must be added the work involved with other necessities of life. The household routine is a major element. The more goods and property we possess, the more time they take. Keeping in mind the time scale noted in the first chapter, it is obvious that nonleisure obligations take up by far the biggest chunk of a person's time, even though some of the items may not be ordinarily considered as work.

The most notable result of this abundance of work is the sense of fatigue that afflicts most working adults. One sociologist of work has stressed "the importance of fatigue in today's urban and industrial civilizations."[7] A study that asked industrial workers what they would do with an extra hour per day found that most of the responses were, "Sleep."[8] In general, fatigue and exhaustion have become the assumed way of life in our society.

In its more acute forms, overwork in the contemporary world has produced the workaholic syndrome. Workaholics are people whose desire to work is compulsive and extreme. People of both sexes and every occupation can be found in the ranks of workaholics. Workaholics think about work even when they are not on the job. They are intense, energetic, competitive, and driven. Workaholics prefer work to leisure, and fear failure, boredom, and laziness. They are incapable of setting limits to their work or of saying "no." They do not delegate well, and they demand a lot from both themselves and others. Finally, although workaholism is often discussed as though it were a disease, most workaholics are satisfied and content with their lives, though their lifestyle does produce problems for people who have to live with them.[9]

Wayne Oates, in his book *Confessions of a Workaholic*, looks at the workaholic syndrome in a religious light.[10] According to Oates, workaholics with a religious orientation practice a religion of solitude and a religion of works and productivity. Not surprisingly, they are preoccupied with thoughts of work even during church services, and they follow the extremes of either not having time for church activities or turning those activities into yet another form of compulsive work.

In recent years we have added not only *workaholic* to our vocabulary but also the dreaded word *burnout*. This too has become the object of sophisticated psychological study and is further evidence of the problem of overwork in our culture.[11] A study of employees in eighteen public and private organizations found that just under half suffered from psychological burnout.[12]

Before we can see how the Christian faith speaks to the problem of too much work we need to ask, What has produced this excessive compulsion to work in our culture? The workaholic syndrome is fed by the twin streams of an acquisitive culture that wants more and more things and a success-oriented culture that wants success at any cost. The mid-eighties coined the term *yuppies* to denote young, upwardly mobile, ambitious people preoccupied with wealth and success. Many of them spend nearly half of their week—close to seventy hours—in their work.[13] These are people for whom work has become an idol. We should note too that this devotion to success has become institutionalized in the form of jobs and professions that require people to be workaholics in order to hold the job.

Dissatisfaction in Work

A second problem with work today is a decline in the satisfaction people feel in their work. The available research focuses on the dissatisfaction of employees with their jobs, but this should not obscure the similar feelings we all have about much of the work that we do as part of the routine *off* the job.

The picture is not equally negative with every occupation. For example, four out of ten professionals and managers reported they were "very satisfied" with their work, while little more than one out of ten unskilled workers responded that positively.[14] The same study showed that whereas professionals would generally choose similar work again, fewer than half of the workers at lower levels would do so.

Other surveys show similar discontent in the workplace. Less than half of a group of blue collar workers claimed to be satisfied with their jobs most of the time.[15] When asked, "What type of work would you try to get into if you could start all over again?" less than half of a cross section of white collar workers and less than one-fourth of a cross section of blue collar workers indicated they would choose the same type of work.[16]

In short, one of the problems of work is that much of it is inherently unsatisfying. In the survey on how Americans use their time, work was mentioned more frequently as the least enjoyable daily activity than as the most enjoyable one.[17] On occasions when I teach the poem in Ecclesiastes about the meaningless cycle of life under the sun (Ecclesiastes 1:4-11), I find that housewives resonate very deeply with the weariness with life expressed by the ancient preacher.

Part of the dissatisfaction with work can be tied to technology and industrialism. The machine and assembly line have introduced a high degree of tedium and stressful jobs into modern industry. Many jobs have become depersonalized, repetitive, and uncreative.

The problems introduced by modern technology often go by the name *alienation in work*. This refers to the way in which work on the assembly line (for example) does not engage the personality of the worker. Workers become alienated from the task they do for a living. One expert diagnoses the problem as having four dimensions:

> *powerlessness* (inability to control the work process), *meaninglessness* (inability to develop a sense of purpose connecting the job to the overall productive process), *isolation* (inability to belong to integrated industrial communities), and *self-estrangement* (failure to become involved in the activity of work as a mode of self-expression).[18]

The Congressional study *Work in America* concluded that "significant numbers of American workers are dissatisfied with the quality of their working lives. Dull, repetitive, seemingly meaningless tasks, offering little challenge or autonomy, are causing discontent among workers at all occupational levels."[19]

Dissatisfaction with one's work takes its final toll in a declining work ethic, a major problem on the work scene today. A healthy work ethic exists when the workers in a society believe in the inherent value of doing good work. But the work ethic in the United States and elsewhere has deteriorated in recent years.

Only one out of four American workers say they are performing to their full capacity. A majority of jobholders, business leaders, and labor-union leaders believe people are not working as hard as they did ten years ago. When one group of workers kept diaries between 1965 and 1975, the results showed that time actually spent working on the job fell by 10 percent. Someone who clocked actual work over a two-year period found that only half of the time on the job was spent working; the other half was spent on coffee breaks, late starts, early quits, waiting, and otherwise idle time.[20]

A 1981 Harris study produced similar results.[21] Three-fourths of all working Americans felt that "people take less pride in their work than they did 10 years ago," and nearly that same number believed that workmanship is worse than it was. And 63 percent felt that "most people do not work as hard today as they did 10 years ago."

A declining work ethic naturally produces poorer work. From time to time the decline in the quality of services receives feature-article coverage in our major news magazines. A study showed that a fourth of American workers are ashamed of the quality of goods they produce, while well over three-fourths of business and government executives believed that the leading factor in diminishing U.S. competitiveness in business is a low commitment to quality products.[22] To find friendly and helpful assistance from clerks in stores has become almost obsolete.

In sum, there seems to be abundant reason to accept one writer's opinion that "there is little more evidence of an active and operative 'work ethic' among American wage earners today than there was in the days of child labor, the sweat shop, and the seventy to eighty hour week."[23]

Unemployment and Underemployment

If too much work is a problem, so is too little work. Unemployment is an economic and social problem that lies beyond the scope of this book, but its reality must be noted. The problems of unemployment are as much psychological as economic. If too much work damages people, so does too little work. A sense of personal worth and feeling of purpose in life depend on a person's ability to work productively.[24]

While statistics on unemployment are ever before us, those on underemployment are not. Yet the underemployed are one of the most numerous groups in the work force today. Underemployed people are those whose work does not match their mental or physical abilities.

The phenomenon of underemployment is tied to the educational level of workers. With increased education go higher abilities and expectations for challenge and reward. One study found that "the most dissatisfied workers are those who are too highly educated for their jobs."[25]

Summary

The problems of overwork, dissatisfaction in work, and not enough work do not exhaust what might be said about the crisis in work today. One thinks of the decline of morality in the workplace and marketplace. The slogan "business is business" covers a multitude of sins, including the tendency of management to stress quantity over quality.

The problems that I have delineated are ones that were once discussed within a context of the Christian religion. They are now regarded in a secular light. The lost province of the Christian religion is itself part of the problem. Most workers today work without a knowledge of the answers that Christianity once provided to the problems of work.

The Leisure Problem

The midtwentieth century gave us the phrase "the leisure problem." The phrase is still accurate, but the writers who popularized the phrase exactly missed the point. It was assumed that we were moving toward shorter and shorter work weeks. The result, predicted the experts, would be that people would not know what to do with themselves when they entered the boundless expanses of leisure. It turns out that the predictions were naively optimistic about the quantity of leisure in the modern world.

Not Enough Leisure

There can be little doubt that the chief problem of leisure today is that there is simply not enough of it. In the opening chapter I gave as a preliminary definition of leisure that it is free time. Leisure viewed as time is exactly where the problem has surfaced.

The assumption that people in our culture have vast amounts of free time is a fallacy. Despite the predictions of futurists, the work week has remained constant since the post-World War II days.[26] One study calculated the amount of free hours per week after people complete work and household chores as twenty to thirty hours.[27] This still leaves a vast array of other obligatory activities to be done. Another survey concluded that of the 168 hours available to people each week, 80 percent were devoted to work, housework, personal needs, and related travel, again not counting some types of obligatory activities.[28]

One of the fallacies that is commonly accepted as truth is that the growth of technology produces an increase in free time. An international study of time usage found that the American city included in the survey, representing the most technologically developed culture in the world, showed a larger amount of working time than cities in other countries.[29] Increased technology in the home produces little reduction in the amount of time spent on household chores, though presumably more things are being done.[30] These statistics are buttressed by the personal observation of E. F. Schumacher, who concluded:

the amount of genuine leisure available in a society is generally in inverse proportion to the amount of labor saving machinery it employs. If you would travel, as I have done, from England to the United States and on to a country like Burma, you would not fail to see the truth of this assertion.[31]

Even more telling than statistics is the thesis of Staffan Linder's book *The Harried Leisure Class.* The argument runs like this. The amount of time we have at our disposal is fixed. An acquisitive and affluent lifestyle such as we currently have tends to take more and more of our time. As the volume of consumption of goods and services increases, so does the time that these things require of us. The net result is a loss of free time. The minimum prerequisite for leisure is free time, but what we increasingly face is a time famine.

To illustrate the accuracy of this diagnosis, consider what happens when a family buys a motorboat. The time on the lake is the leisure goal. But look at the surrounding activities that gobble up leisure time. The boat must be cleaned and maintained. It requires gasoline and battery upkeep. It has to be cleaned in the spring and put away for winter storage. Traveling to and from the lake takes time. In fact, the more people around who can afford boats, the slower will be the traffic around the lake. To afford the boat in the first place may have required a wage earner whose work is far in excess of a forty-hour per week job. Other things being equal, a family without a boat will actually have more leisure time than the family with the boat.

What we see here on a small scale is happening in our society on a grand scale. The time commitment that our consumption requires snatches away the very leisure we thought we were gaining. The more things we have, the larger house we need, the more time we spend maintaining the things, and the less time we have to enjoy leisure. The crowning irony is that most people in our culture acquire more articles than they have time to use. Technology enlarges the possibilities of leisure but in most people's lives it actually decreases the amount of leisure.

The theory of a harried leisure class has been extended by Geoffrey Godbey. If we agree that leisure by definition includes an attitude of freedom from coercion, then much of what we think to be leisure is actually antileisure. Writes Godbey,

> By anti-leisure I refer to activity which is undertaken compulsively, as a means to an end, for a perception of necessity, with a high degree of externally composed constraints, with considerable anxiety, with a high degree of time consciousness, with a minimum of personal autonomy. . . .[32]

A prime example is the obsessive drive of middle and upper class families to cater to their children's activities during the growing up years. Life becomes a blur as parents see to it that their children participate in sports, music, school activities, church events, and social events. As parents make sure they do not fail their children, leisure drops out of their lives.

An overstimulated lifestyle is rushed and therefore unleisurely. The best confirmation that our very lifestyle adds up to a lack of leisure is a study that asked respondents how often they felt rushed to complete their day's activities. One-fourth said they "always feel rushed," 53 percent said they "sometimes feel rushed," and only 22 percent said they "almost never feel rushed."[33]

Poor Quality of Leisure

Not only do many people in our culture lack sufficient time for leisure, but there has also been a decline in the quality of leisure life. In making this indictment I am of course revealing my own sense of values. Leisure always involves the question of our values.

It is not surprising, therefore, that the decline of moral and intellectual values in our culture should be reflected in how people spend their leisure time. The moral and intellectual content of most people's leisure pursuits is alarmingly low. The cultural malaise that Paul Elmen has analyzed in his book *The Restoration of Meaning to Contemporary Life* is fully evident in how most people spend their leisure time: boredom, the search for distraction, the fear of spending time by oneself, sensuality, escape into comedy, violence, and the appeal of horror ("the fun of being frightened").[34]

Leisure is more than nonwork. It is an actively chosen, positive use of time. Judged by such a standard, much of what passes for leisure is less than leisure. One authority cites studies of young people that show "how drab, monotonous, dull and boring" spare time is for them.[35] Someone else has written about a "leisure lack," meaning a lack of leisure "understood as a state of mind."[36] In one study, only 17 percent of an urban sample included leisure as one of the three most important aspects of their life making for satisfaction or dissatisfaction, while the author of another survey "was struck by the slight importance of leisure activity" in the lives of workers.[37]

The technological revolution has contributed to a decline in the quality of leisure. For one thing, as Linder argues in *The Harried Leisure Class*, in a consumer society people want more and more things. Given the scarcity of time, the time allotted to each leisure activity declines. People do not simply listen to music, for example. Music is background for some other activity. For the amateur photographer, the need to get good pictures competes with the leisure function of visiting a site. In short, the competition of leisure pursuits for our time has diluted the quality of our leisure. The leisure aspect of the lunch or dinner table, the delights of conversation, and the capacity to enjoy beauty are prime examples.

Cultural pursuits have also been hard hit by the competition for time. Reading has declined drastically from even three decades ago. A Gallup poll found that 58 percent of Americans have never finished reading a book, while a survey commissioned by a book industry study group similarly revealed that nearly half of Americans never read a book of any type.[38] The international study of time usage confirmed that Americans read far less than Europeans.[39]

All of which brings us to the subject of television. It accounts for nearly half of leisure time in America, and for 40 percent of the time not devoted to sleep, employment, and family and personal care.[40]

Aside from the fact that television viewing has replaced more worthwhile leisure activities, it is open to criticism for the passivity that accompanies it as a leisure pursuit. If we define leisure in terms of activity and oppose it to idleness or mere time killing, much television viewing is hard pressed to rate as leisure. Psychologists have documented the trancelike fixation of television viewers that destroys the ability to engage in conscious thought. Studies of brainwave activity have shown how inactive the brain is while a person watches television.[41]

The most significant recent critique of television is Neil Postman's book *Amusing Ourselves to Death*.[42] Postman shows that in contrast to written and oral discourse, television encourages passivity, incoherence (lack of ability to conduct sustained thinking on a subject), lack of deliberation, and triviality. It floods us with information with which we are expected to do nothing. What we get from television lacks action value and therefore produces a sense of impotency. As a medium, moreover, television has produced a world of broken time and broken attention.

I do not wish to give the impression that television by itself produced the mindlessness and emptiness of much modern leisure. Television would never have proven so popular as a pastime if it were not for the prevailing fatigue we noted earlier in our discussion of overwork. Most people lack the physical energy to do anything other than plop down in front of the television. Furthermore, the American preference for recreation over culture (broadly defined) has undermined the intellectual and cultural content of leisure as much as television has.

Inability to Value Leisure Apart from Work

A third difficulty with leisure today is that it is often valued only in relation to work. This is the syndrome of a utilitarian play ethic that always ends up robbing play or leisure of any intrinsic value. In this view, leisure is of value only as it contributes to work. In our culture, which generally over-values work and success, this has been the fate of leisure. As Robert Johnston puts it, "Leisure is not viewed as an independent occurrence, or even a complementary activity. Rather, it is placed under the tyranny of a work mentality."[43]

Work can thus be an obstacle to leisure, even when it does not actually prevent us from engaging in leisure pursuits. Leisure pursued under the constant pressure of knowing that one is taking time from the obligations of work is barely leisure at all. Workaholics blur the distinction between work and leisure, turning work into their hobby and losing the quality of leisure that stems from its contrast to work.[44] In the words of William Whyte, "They are never less at leisure than when they are at leisure."[45] At the opposite extreme are workaholics who find leisure time so unstructured that they become lethargic and passive in their free time.[46]

The final result of valuing leisure only as an aid to work is to make leisure like work. People carry over into leisure the same drive for productivity that they require of work. Many sporting activities have more in common with rigorous work than with leisure. In fact, any leisure activity will, if pursued with the compulsion of work, become just another form of work. One authority claims that "more and more we work at our play. . . . We begin to evaluate our leisure in terms of the potential it has for work."[47] This probably explains why many achievers cannot genuinely enjoy leisure.

Guilt Over the Enjoyment of Leisure

It is an easy step from a utilitarian attitude toward leisure to the inability to enjoy leisure. The reasons for this are multiple. One is the workaholic syndrome that prevents workers from experiencing leisure as leisure. Even on vacations they want to "stay on top of the job," and so they never leave the job behind. Alternately, they pursue leisure activities with the same competitive drive with which they do their work.

Another facet of the inability to enjoy leisure is the guilt many in our culture feel about doing something other than working. Among a certain segment of the population, leisure is viewed as unproductive, of little value to society, and evidence of being privileged.

The fact that we live in a permissive and hedonistic society sometimes conceals the presence of the opposite attitude. Psychologists call it *anhedonia*—the inability to feel pleasure—and regard it as an abnormality in personality. Applied to leisure, we are talking about people who, in the words of one book title, feel guilty when they relax.[48] An added irony is that some of the very people who feel guilty when they take time for leisure are often the same people who feel guilty because they work too much.

It is not surprising, therefore, that someone wrote a book entitled *The Decline of Pleasure*.[49] The thesis obviously does not fit everyone, but it fits a significant percentage of the population. Our culture, writes the author, overvalues what is useful, with the result that "we go to our pleasures, when we dare go to them at all, demanding that they surrender to us a kind of knowledge that is not in them. And so we kill them." Unable to invest the pleasure of things and activities with an inherent value, many people in our society miss the pleasure they can give.

As an example of how the utilitarian impulse can destroy the pleasure of leisure, Kerr cites an experience recounted by the British writer Christopher Fry. Fry once went to see a play, not as a member of the audience, but because he had to write a review of the performance. Recalls Fry, "I could scarcely hear a word of the play for the noise of my own mind wondering how I should write about it."[50]

Leisure as Idolatry

The final leisure problem stands in contrast to what I have said thus far. Not enough time for leisure, inability actively to choose high-quality leisure pursuits, leisure as an appendage to work, guilt about enjoying the pleasures of leisure—these are the results of undervaluing leisure. But for a sizable minority in our culture, the opposite abuse is true. They are the ones who overvalue leisure and often turn it into an idol. Let us not overlook that if there are workaholics in our culture, there are also golfaholics, jogaholics, television junkies, and rock music addicts.

This overvaluing of leisure takes several forms. One is the self-indulgence that leads some people to spend virtually all of their nonworking time and resources on having fun. There is no time left for helping others, or for worshiping God. Leisure pursuits can tyrannize not only one's time but also one's money.

Another manifestation of this obsession with leisure is the endless weekend—not only living for the weekend but also talking about it all week long. Or, if not the weekend, then the after-work leisure activities.

If an excessive devotion to work can rob leisure of its joy and meaning, the reverse is also possible, with excessive devotion to leisure detracting from the value of work. For many Americans, work has ceased to have intrinsic value and has been reduced to that which makes the weekend—or the social standing of one's family—possible.

An additional facet of this problem is the way in which urban living and the orientation of family living around the children have made young people the leisure class of today. Farm life once provided an early transition from play to work for adolescents and early teenagers. Today young people begin working later. The result is that their need to be entertained is excessive and insatiable.

Summary

The problem of leisure is partly that we do not understand it very well. Our cultural value system is dominated by work, and our morality places a premium on efficiency. When placed into such a context, leisure fares poorly. People find too little time for leisure. They gravitate to mediocrity in leisure pursuits, and they are unable to enjoy the pleasures of leisure without guilt feelings. For others in our society, the abuse has been to turn leisure into a god or a rival religion to the Christian faith.

WHAT THE SECULAR SOURCES DON'T TELL YOU

The problems of work and leisure that I have covered are general social problems. They relate to people in our culture regardless of their religious stance. But as I immersed myself in the secular sources, I was continuously left with the feeling that the authorities are oblivious to the religious segment of the population.

For example, in all the time usage surveys that I read, only one included a category for religious activities. This leaves the impression that the experts presupposed a population for whom Sunday was either a working day or a holiday, but certainly not a holy day. If one is looking for an index to the prevailingly secular bias in scholarship, a glance at the sociological sources on work and leisure will suffice.

What, then, happens when we look at the problems of work and leisure as applied to Christians? My conclusion is that the problems we have noted are even more acute for Christians than they are for the population at large.

To begin, consider how much time is taken up with religious activities. Christian living at once adds time commitments for prayer, devotional reading, church attendance, Bible studies, committee work, volunteer work in the church or for Christian agencies, and so on. The general tendency is for these activities to take time away from potential leisure time and increase the time spent at the obligatory end of the time scale. The problems of overwork and inadequate leisure tend to be heightened at once for Christians.

Then, too, there is the Christian ideal of service to those in need. When taken seriously, this places further strain on the daily time budget, and we can chalk up another victory for the antileisure side. This is reinforced by a bias in favor of self-discipline and self-sacrifice, which often translates into a distrust of pleasure or enjoyment. A recent study of evangelical Protestants noted that they "have tended to value productive or constructive activities in their leisure (e.g., volunteer work, working around the house, taking courses, and gardening)."[51] To this we can add the duty that Christians feel toward contributing a portion of their money to religious causes, thereby decreasing the amount of money available for leisure and perhaps increasing the need for additional income.

The net result is to make the impulse toward overwork and the time famine for leisure even more acute for Christians. I do not wish to deny that Christianity also contains within itself the seeds for resolving these problems, but we need to note at the outset that the problems of work and leisure are often even more severe among Christians than among the general population.

FURTHER READING

Georges Friedmann, *The Anatomy of Work: Labor, Leisure, and the Implications of Automation* (1961).

Erwin O. Smigel, ed. *Work and Leisure: A Contemporary Social Problem* (1963).

Staffan Linder, *The Harried Leisure Class* (1970).

Studs Terkel, *Working: People Talk about What They Do All Day and How They Feel about What They Do* (1972).

Marilyn Machlowitz, *Workaholics: Living with Them, Working with Them* (1980).

Chapter 2, Notes

1. Studs Terkel, *Working: People Talk about What They Do All Day and How They Feel about What They Do* (New York: Pantheon Books, 1972).

2. John P. Robinson, *How Americans Use Their Time: A Social Psychological Analysis of Everyday Behavior* (New York: Praeger Publishers, 1977), 48.

3. Harold L. Wilensky, "The Uneven Distribution of Leisure: The Impact of Economic Growth on 'Free Time,' " in *Work and Leisure: A Contemporary Social Problem*, ed. Erwin O. Smigel (New Haven, Conn.: College and University Press, 1963), 136.

4. Geoffrey Godbey, *Leisure in Your Life: An Exploration* (Philadelphia: Saunders College, 1980), 106.

5. Stanley Parker, *The Sociology of Leisure* (New York: International Publications Service, 1976), 67.

6. Robert K. Johnston, *The Christian at Play* (Grand Rapids, Mich.: Wm. B. Eerdmans Publishing Co., 1983), 11.

7. Joffre Dumazedier, *Toward a Society of Leisure*, trans. Stewart E. McClure (New York: Free Press, 1967), 81.

8. Robert S. Weiss and David Riesman, "Some Issues in the Future of Leisure," in *Work and Leisure*, 172.

9. Marilyn Machlowitz, *Workaholics: Living with Them, Working with Them* (Reading, Mass.: Addison-Wesley Publishing Co., 1980).

10. Wayne Oates, *Confessions of a Workaholic: The Facts about Work Addiction* (New York: World, 1971).

11. See Whiton Steward Paine, ed., *Job Stress and Burnout: Research, Theory, and Intervention Perspectives* (Beverly Hills, Calif.: Sage Publications, 1982); and Christina Maslach, *Burnout: The Cost of Caring* (Englewood Cliffs, N.J.: Prentice-Hall, 1982).

12. Muriel Dobbin, "Is the Daily Grind Wearing You Down?" *U. S. News and World Report*, 24 March 1986, 76.

13. Richard Phillips, "The New Calvinists," *Chicago Tribune*, 5 November 1986, sec.7, pp. 5-8.

14. Robert L. Kahn, "The Meaning of Work," in *The Human Meaning of Social Change*, ed. Angus C. Campbell and Philip E. Converse (New York: Russell Sage Foundation, 1972), 182.

15. *Work in America* [report of a task force to the Secretary of Health, Education, and Welfare] (Cambridge, Mass.: MIT Press, 1973), 15.

16. Ibid.

17. Noted by John Neulinger, *The Psychology of Leisure*, 2d ed. (Springfield, Ill.: Charles C. Thomas, 1981), 89.

18. Robert Blauner, as summarized by Stanley Parker, *Leisure and Work* (London: George Allen and Unwin, 1983), 31. Blauner's book is entitled *Alienation and Freedom: The Factory Worker and His Industry* (Chicago: University of Chicago Press, 1964).

19. *Work in America*, xv.

20. Daniel Yankelovich and John Immerwahr, "Putting the Work Ethic to Work," *Society*, January-February 1984, 58-76.

21. Daniel Yankelovich, "The Work Ethic Is Underemployed," *Psychology Today*, May 1982, 6.

22. Yankelovich and Immerwahr, 72.

23. John R. Kelly, *Leisure* (Englewood Cliffs, N.J.: Prentice-Hall, 1982), 117.

24. For more on the problems of the unemployed, see John C. Raines and Donna C. Day-Lower, *Modern Work and Human Meaning* (Philadelphia: Westminster Press, 1986).

25. Godbey, 107.

26. Staffan Linder, *The Harried Leisure Class* (New York: Columbia University Press, 1970), 135.

27. Dumazedier, 93.

28. Robinson, 89.

29. Alexander Szalai, ed., *The Use of Time: Daily Activities of Urban and Suburban Populations in Twelve Countries* (The Hague: Mouton, 1972), 464.

30. Ibid., 126.

31. E. F. Schumacher, *Good Work* (New York: Harper and Row, 1979), 25.

32. Geoffrey Godbey, "Anti-leisure and Public Recreation Policy," in S. R. Parker et al., *Sport and Leisure in Contemporary Society* (London: Polytechnic of Central London, 1975), 47.

33. Robinson, 133.

34. Paul Elmen, *The Restoration of Meaning to Contemporary Life*, (Garden City, N.Y.: Doubleday, 1958).

35. Kenneth Roberts, *Contemporary Society and the Growth of Leisure* (London: Longman, 1978), 24.

36. Neulinger, 213.

37. Parker, 147.

38. Arthur Schlesinger, Jr., "Implications of Leisure for Government," in *Technology, Human Values, and Leisure*, ed. Max Kaplan and Phillip Bosserman (Nashville: Abingdon Press, 1971), 77; Herbert Mitgan, "Study Finds Nearly Half of U.S. Do Not Read Books," *New York Times*, 14 November 1978, 13.

39. Szalai, 283.q; 40. Godbey, 85; John R. Kelly, *Leisure Identities and Interactions* (London: George Allen and Unwin, 1983), 131.

40. Godbey, 85; John R. Kelly, *Leisure Identities and Interactions* (London: George Allen and Unwin, 1983), 131.

41. See, for example, Jerry Mander, *Four Arguments for the Elimination of Television* (New York: William Morrow and Co., 1964).

42. Neil Postman, *Amusing Ourselves to Death: Public Discourse in the Age of Show Business* (New York: Viking Press, 1985).

43. Johnston, 21.

44. Machlowitz, 87-101.

45. William H. Whyte, Jr., *The Organization Man* (New York: Simon and Schuster, 1956), 150.

46. Machlowitz, 87.

47. Gregory P. Stone, "American Sports: Play and Display," in Eric Larrabee and Rolf Meyersohn, eds., *Mass Leisure* (Glencoe: Free Press, 1958), 258.

48. Tim Hansel, *When I Relax I Feel Guilty* (Elgin, Ill.: David C. Cook Publishing Co., 1979).

49. Walter Kerr, *The Decline of Pleasure* (New York: Simon and Schuster, 1962).

50. Ibid., 234.

51. James Davison Hunter, *Evangelicalism: The Coming Generation* (Chicago: University of Chicago Press, 1987), 52.

Chapter 3

A History of Attitudes toward Work and Leisure

*T*here are several reasons why it is worth our time to take a brief excursion through the history of attitudes toward work and leisure. We cannot afford the naivete of beginning anew with each generation. There are lessons to be learned from the past that will help us in the present. Furthermore, the history I am about to summarize provides yet another agenda of issues that helps us understand the contemporary scene to which the Christian faith speaks.

My overview of how the human race has regarded work and leisure is not a history of work and leisure but of *attitudes toward* work and leisure. To gauge the extent to which ordinary people practiced what the thinkers of their day said is beyond the scope of this book.

A HISTORY OF ATTITUDES TOWARD WORK

Western culture rests on two foundations—the classical (Greco-Roman) and biblical (Judeo-Christian). Since I accept the Bible as the authority for belief and practice, it is in a sense the main concern of this book. I will therefore save the biblical data for later.

The Classical View of Work: The Unworthiness of Labor

The status of work got off to an inauspicious start in ancient Greece and Rome.[1] To the Greeks, work was a curse and something beneath the dignity of a free person. Their word for it was taken from the same root that produced the word sorrow. Physical work, especially, was regarded as degrading to human dignity.

Aristotle is a main spokesman for the Greek attitude. For him, leisure was the goal of life. Since physical labor is an obstacle to such leisure, it is unworthy of a free person. To lead the life of a craftsman or trader is to lead a life "devoid of nobility and hostile to perfection of character."

According to Xenophon, Socrates held a similar view of work:

> The mechanical arts carry a social stigma and are rightly dishonored in our cities. For these arts can damage the bodies of those who work at them. . . . This physical degeneration results also in deterioration of the soul. Furthermore, the workers at these trades simply have not got the time to perform the offices of friendship or citizenship. Consequently they are looked upon as bad friends and bad patriots.

Here again we see the Greek urge for freedom. To labor is to be enslaved by necessity. It is not the work alone that is bad, but also the idea of giving up one's independence to work for someone else—or out of physical necessity. In such a view, the only way to redeem the curse of work was to avoid work. The whole Greek social structure helped to support such an outlook, for it rested on the premise that slaves and artisans did the work, enabling the elite to devote themselves to the exercise of the mind in art, philosophy, and politics.

The poet Hesiod expressed the Greek attitude in mythological form. Work, he said, originated with Eris, goddess of strife, while labor, along with other evils, came from Pandora's box and was a punishment from Zeus.

Work fared only slightly better in Roman antiquity. Whereas in our own work-oriented society we define leisure as nonwork, the Romans reversed the matter. Their word for work was *negotium*, meaning "nonleisure." In such a climate of opinion, it is not surprising that Cicero wrote,

> The toil of a hired worker, who is paid only for his toil and not for artistic skill, is unworthy of a free man and is sordid in character. . . . Trade on a small retail scale is also sordid.

Before we leave the classical disparagement of work, we should note that it was based not only on a social structure of slavery but was also rooted in the philosophy of the age. In general, classical philosophy held a low view of the physical world. If, as Seneca put it, the body is necessary rather than important and "to despise our bodies is pure freedom," it is obvious that physical work undertaken to supply the needs of the body in this world would be disparaged.

The Middle Ages and the Sacred-Secular Dichotomy

The main contribution of the Middle Ages to the history of attitudes toward work was to divide work into two great categories: the sacred and the secular. The roots of such an attitude were already present in the classical social distinction between free people and slaves. The Middle Ages simply gave this hierarchy a spiritual cast.

Postbiblical Hebraism exalted the contemplative religious life at the expense of physical labor. The school of Rabbi Simeon condemned physical work because it took time from the spiritual life. If people would only do the will of God, ran the argument, their work would be done by others.[2]

A similar distinction can be found in a prayer of the Jewish Talmud in which the rabbi prayed,

> I thank thee, O Lord, my God, that thou hast given me my lot with those who sit in the house of learning, and not with those who sit at the street-corners; for

> I am early to work and they are early to work; I am
> early to work on the words of the Torah, and they
> are early to work on things of no moment. I weary
> myself, and they weary themselves; I weary myself
> and profit thereby, and they weary themselves to no
> profit. I run, and they run; I run towards the life of
> the age to come, and they run towards the pit of
> destruction.[3]

The result of this division into sacred and secular was of course
to reduce ordinary workers to second-class spiritual citizens.

The same division of work into categories of sacred and
secular became a leading feature of medieval Roman Catholicism. This attitude was reflected by Eusebius in the fourth
century:

> Two ways of life were given by the law of Christ
> to His Church. The one is above nature, and beyond
> common human living. . . . Wholly and perma-
> nently separate from the common customary life of
> mankind, it devotes itself to the service of God
> alone. . . . Such then is the perfect form of the
> Christian life. And the other, more humble, more
> human, permits men to . . . have minds for farming,
> for trade, and the other more secular interests as
> well as for religion. . . . And a kind of secondary
> grade of piety is attributed to them.[4]

The difference between the two types of work was not a difference of degree but of kind. As one authority describes the
situation, "Within the monastery or convent, the 'religious'
who . . . aimed at perfection devoted themselves largely
(though not exclusively) to contemplation, while outside in the
family, in the market place, in the field and on the seas, the
others kept the wheels of the work of the world running, at
the cost of condemning their souls to a second-best spiritual
life."[5]

This division of work into sacred and secular was the chief legacy the Middle Ages bequeathed to the world on the subject of work. It has led a vigorous life ever since and persists today, not only in Catholic circles but in conservative Protestant ones as well.

There were, of course, other developments during the Middle Ages. In some quarters work became an extension of an ascetic outlook. In this tradition, people worked, not because work had inherent dignity in the sight of God, but for the opposite reason—it was painful and humiliating and therefore meritorious as an act of atonement.[6]

Physical work was also prescribed for those living in monasteries, but we should not romanticize this as something that dignified work in general. For one thing, the bulk of the daily schedule was devoted to the contemplative life, not to active work. Furthermore, it was done within the confines of the monastery and did not extend to work done in the world. As the best-known modern history of attitudes toward work notes, monastic work "is never exalted as anything of value in itself, but only as an instrument of purification, of charity, of expiation. . . . The work done by outsiders in the great world is regarded with indulgent charity but is in no way honored."[7]

This negative picture of work in the world was slightly mitigated as the Catholic church made concessions toward the reality of what was happening in society. Thomas Aquinas, for example, affirmed work as a natural right and duty. He drew up a hierarchy of professions and trades, thereby lending a sanction to what was happening in the social order in which he lived. But Thomas perpetuates the preference for the contemplative life over active work.[8]

The Renaissance and Reformation: The Dignity of Life's Work

Historians are so preoccupied with what the Reformation did to revolutionize work that they act as though the Renaissance did not even occur. This is surely an oversight. The flowering of humanism that we call the Renaissance asserted the dignity of life's labors and especially valued the work of one's hands.

This attitude breathes through the masterpiece of English Renaissance humanism, Thomas More's *Utopia* (1516). Written by a Catholic, the work expresses a Renaissance attitude toward work. In More's "Nowhere" (which is what "utopia" means), people work only six hours a day—not because they despise work, but in order to "give all citizens as much time as public needs permit for freeing and developing their minds." As for physical work, all adults—men and women alike—work equally. In fact, jobs are rotated to insure equality. In this ideal commonwealth, "no loafing is tolerated," and More goes out of his way to pay his disrespects to the "multitude of priests and so-called religious men, as numerous as they are idle," that afflicted European society at the time.

A modern historian writes this about the influence of the Renaissance on attitudes toward work:

> Their idea of work expresses their confidence and
> exuberance. Unwittingly, it sings the praises of the
> kind of work at which they excelled—the individual,
> craftsmanlike, artistic. . . . Their work required that
> hands touch materials. It was this non-agricultural
> manual labor they rescued from the contempt in
> which the ancient world had left it. They gave work
> the dignity the word craftsmanship carries still.[9]

Even more decisive, however, was the influence of Luther, Calvin, and the Puritans. The "Protestant work ethic" has been the subject of so much distortion that I will devote a separate chapter to it. For purposes of this historical sketch, therefore, I will be content to summarize what the sixteenth and seventeenth centuries contributed to thought about work.

The Reformers began by rejecting the medieval division of work into sacred and secular. To this they added the doctrine of vocation or calling, by which they meant that God called people to tasks in the world. The result of this was to make all work done for God's glory sacred. The dignity of common work never stood higher than at this moment in history. This holy worldliness also found a place for industriousness as a lifestyle and profit as a motive for work, although the Reformers did preach a sense of moderation in lifestyle. All of this affirmation of work and earthly endeavor of course presupposed a spiritual context in which the godly life was valued supremely and in which no work was divorced from the idea of service to God and others.

If the classical disparagement of work was an extension of the classical world view, so was the Protestant attitude. The cornerstone of Protestant thought was the sovereignty of God in all of life. From this flowed an awareness of God's creation of the world and his providential concern for it. Given this affirmation of the world in which God has placed his creatures as stewards, it was inevitable that the Reformation tradition attached dignity to human work in the world.

The Enlightenment: Secularizing the Protestant Work Ethic

The next chapter in the history of attitudes toward work is the saddest of all. It consisted of gradually removing the Protestant work ethic from its Christian context. Without the restraining influence of Protestant belief in the primacy of the spiritual, the tenets of the original Protestant ethic became perverted into a creed of personal success. This secularized perversion is what most people today mean when they speak glibly of "the Protestant ethic." The truth is that the people of the Reformation era would be horrified by what goes under the banner of "the Protestant ethic."

This eighteenth-century development is expressed best by Benjamin Franklin, whose *Poor Richard* proverbs show us what a secularized Protestant ethic looks like. [10] We might first note what is not present. We do not find a conviction that the purpose of life and work is to glorify God and enjoy him forever. Also gone are the ideas of work as stewardship of what

God has given to his creatures and the moral duty to help those in need.

In the place of these we find an ethic of self-interest and expediency. Sloth, for example, is shunned because it brings diseases and shortens life. Or consider the following Franklin aphorisms:

Industry pays debts.

Early to bed, and early to rise,
makes a man healthy, wealthy, and wise.

He that hath a calling hath an office
of profit and honor.

God helps them that help themselves.

Here, indeed, is the exaltation of a humanistic ethic, ordering human affairs apart from God's grace. Franklin's quip that God gives all things to industry epitomizes this God-on-a-string mentality.

What comes through most strongly is a preoccupation with money and getting ahead. Work is only a means to that end, and life itself is ceaseless work, with no time for leisure or worship. *Be ashamed to catch yourself idle*, says Poor Richard. Again, *Leisure is time for doing something useful.* This hoarding of time spent in work is matched by a hoarding of one's money: *If you would be wealthy, think of saving as well as of getting.*

I trust it is obvious that when a modern writer talks about "the decline of the Protestant ethic," he is actually talking about the humanistic ethic of the eighteenth century.[11] This is evident from the traits he ascribes to it: survival of the fittest, thrift, social climbing based on economic success, self-denying work, and self-reliance.

The names of Adam Smith and John Locke might be added to the list of spokesmen for the new work ethic based on economic self-interest. In *The Wealth of Nations*, Smith begins from the premise that it is not from the benevolence of the butcher, the brewer, or the baker that we expect our dinner, but from their regard to their own interest. We address ourselves, not to their humanity but to their self-love.[12]

On this foundation Smith builds his theory, still with us, of a market system based on the law of supply and demand. We have obviously left the Puritan world of Christian stewardship and compassion and entered an economic world governed by the mechanism of economic expediency.

John Locke's views of property as the foundation of society fit into this same framework.[13] Labor itself, when joined with nature, produces the property to which people are entitled by natural right. According to Locke, the thing that makes an acre of land valuable or worthless is the amount of human labor that has been expended to make it profitable. Work, in this view, is valued because it is useful, profitable, and the means for acquiring property. In Locke's view, this process of acquisition is what produced the institution of money.

In North America, immigration became an additional ingredient in the growing secularization of the original Protestant ethic. The immigration ethic is based on the principle that hard work and sacrifice will improve the lot of the next generation. This too is an ethic of self-interest, but at the family level. One writer correctly notes that "for millions of Americans, . . . the immigrant work ethic came at last to merge with the Protestant work ethic."[14]

Modern historians call the eighteenth century "the Enlightenment," but when viewed from the perspective of a Christian work ethic, it was a dark shadow. It replaced a spiritually controlled work ethic with a humanly governed economic system that regarded work as a means to financial ends. Even during the two centuries of the Reformation and Puritan influence there had been a movement in this direction, but with the eighteenth century the floodgates were opened.[15]

The Nineteenth Century: Responses to the Industrial Revolution

The view of Locke and Smith that work is the beginning of wealth produced its inevitable results in the next century, the era of the industrial revolution. Attitudes toward work can best be viewed as responses to the crisis engendered by that revolution.

The crisis is easy to identify. The triumph of the machine greatly accelerated the division of labor into specialized tasks. The growth of factories also heightened the division between owners and laborers, both of whom were driven by the profit motive. In fact, a key question became, Who owns labor—society, industry, or the individual?

For the laborer, specialization produced the phenomenon known today as the alienation of the worker. Its features included the following: narrowness and monotony of tasks, bypassing of trained skill (lack of skill required for tasks), inability to see an overall purpose in one's isolated task, denial of the satisfaction that comes from complexity in work, the depersonalized and anonymous nature of work, the sense of never completing a job, lack of a sense of participation, loss of interest in one's task, and loss of pride in one's work.[16]

The nineteenth century produced two chief answers to these problems, and so far as I can tell, Christian thinkers did not contribute significantly to the dialogue. The dominant answer was Marxism or socialism. The Marxist diagnosis of the problem was accurate, no matter how much we may disagree with its proposed solutions.

Alienation in work was the problem, and it arose from inadequate views of work. When work is viewed as an economic commodity that is bought and sold, exploitation is a natural result unless other factors are strong enough to counter it. Exploitation emerges from the division between owner or manager and laborer. If profit is the motive, the owner will naturally try to make as much profit as possible. The worker becomes like a machine, condemned to a life of forced labor. This is the curse from which Marx sought to free the laborer.

We should notice that Marxism in theory has a high view of work. Work becomes the means by which people find their meaning in life. With an idealized view of what work should be, Marxism was fired by a sense of protest against what the industrial society was in the process of producing. Engels protested against the demoralization of English textile workers:

> Nothing is more terrible than being constrained to do some one thing every day from morning until night against one's will. . . . Why does he work? For love of work? From a natural impulse? Not at all! He works for money, for a thing which has nothing whatsoever to do with the work itself.[17]

Similarly, Marx's discussion of the estrangement of the worker under capitalism was fired by a high view of what work can and should be.[18] For Marx, work "is the very touchstone for man's self-realization," and the thing "which should make him happy."[19]

In its diagnosis of the problems of work in the industrial society, Marxism deserves to be taken seriously. Christian thinking about work cannot afford to ignore the problems Marxism uncovers. When Marx indicts the world for having made money "the god of this world," he asserts a Christian principle.[20]

The Marxist solution on the other hand is too institutional to win the confidence of Christians. It places its hope in a working class that will redeem society. In the words of Marx,

> A class must be formed which . . . is the dissolution of all classes, a sphere of society which has a universal character because its sufferings are universal. . . . This dissolution of society . . . is the *proletariat*.[21]

This is the collectivist answer to the problem of work in an industrial society. Its lack of success in Communist countries tends to conceal insights about the problems of work that are important to an understanding of work in the modern world.

A second response to the industrial revolution of the nineteenth century was the "Romantic" response of idealizing work. Looking back, we can see this attitude as part of Victorian optimism and nostalgia for the past. Sensing that industrial work was dehumanizing, these Romanticists urged a return to something more natural. They valued craftsmanship and the work of one's hands. In some ways they were forerunners of the "simple lifers" of our own century.

The foremost spokesmen for this tradition were John Ruskin and Thomas Carlyle. They exalted the work of one's hands as the Puritans had done, but without the surrounding theological framework. Ruskin wanted to revive the values of earlier centuries when individual craftsmen could express their ability through their work. His follower William Morris called it "work pleasure." Protesting that the phenomenon of the division of labor was wrongly named ("it is not, truly speaking, the labor that is divided; but the men"), Ruskin longed for a society in which "the dishonor of manual labor" would be "done away with altogether."[22]

Ruskin's fellow Victorian Thomas Carlyle could hardly control his enthusiasm for work:

> There is a perennial nobleness, and even sacredness, in Work. . . . The latest Gospel in this world is, Know thy work and do it. . . . Even in the meanest sorts of Labour, the whole soul of a man is composed into a kind of real harmony. . . . All true Work is Religion. . . . All true Work is sacred; in all true Work, were it but true hand labour, there is something of divineness.[23]

If we ask *why* work is this great, the answer is apparently, "It just is."

This is the Victorian exaltation of work. It goes by the name of "Puritanism," but this is a misnomer. Writers such as Ruskin and Carlyle valued work in itself, not work as service to God and society. They idealized the work of the craftsman but did not have much to say to the worker who continued to slave away in the factory.

The Twentieth-Century: The Secular Wasteland

No single attitude toward work dominates the present century, but the various viewpoints tend to share a secular bias. Work is no longer discussed in a religious context. Whereas theologians were once the people to theorize about work, in our century the discussion is largely conducted by economists and sociologists. Within this secular context, the population is divided into a range of attitudes.

The eight-to-five laborer and housewife generally resign themselves to work as necessary evil. Whatever satisfactions life offers, they are more likely to come from family and other home amenities than from work itself. One study, for example, found that only one out of four workers regarded their jobs as a central life interest.[24] For all the dislike of ordinary work, however, no revolution lurks around the corner. These workers have become acclimated to unfulfilling work as the thing that makes the weekend and family life possible.

Among professional classes, work is often an idol. The "organization worker," as well as the self-employed professional, tend to devote an inordinate amount of their weekly schedule to work.[25] These workers tend to be motivated by self-interest and the ideal of upward social mobility based on wealth. Work is carried out within a framework of the success ethic.

Of course the "simple life" rejection of the rat race continues to appeal to a small minority within American society. These are belated "Romanticists," heirs to the nature lovers of the nineteenth century who sought to escape from the mechanization of industrial and urban life.

Finally, we should not overlook the continuing appeal of Marxism around the globe, if not in the United States. While its solutions have not liberated the worker as envisioned, the continuing vitality of Marxism as a philosophic position shows that the problems it addresses are still around. Any adequate work ethic today must take into account the problems of work under capitalism.

Although attitudes toward work are in disarray in our century, we should not conclude that the work ethic is dead. When it expresses itself, however, it is in a secular context. This is epitomized by Richard Nixon's often-quoted Labor Day Message of 6 September 1971:

> Let the detractors of America, the doubters of the American spirit, take note. America's competitive spirit, the work ethic of this people, is alive and well on Labor Day, 1971. The dignity of work, the value of achievement, the morality of self-reliance— none of these is going out of style.[26]

What the Historical Survey Tells Us

There are several lessons to be learned from the history of attitudes toward work. The ease with which the human race has fallen into inadequate views of work shows that it is a subject that requires careful thought. To reach the right position on work does not occur naturally and spontaneously. Indeed, one is impressed by how much heartache has been visited on people through the centuries by bad doctrines of work.

The history of attitudes toward work is also a roadmap to the dead ends that face us in our own cultural setting. We too can undervalue or disdain earthly work. We too can wrongly decide that "full-time Christian service" is spiritually more distinguished than washing the dishes or working the eight-to-five shift. We can likewise slip into the errors of divorcing work from its context of Christian service to God and others, or making an idol of it, or performing it as a necessary evil.

We should notice, too, that every age has tended to make its view of work conform to prevailing social practices. In a society based on slavery, Greek thinkers decided that work was beneath the dignity of free people. In an era when the clergy dominated society, people were content with a two-track view of work that made ordinary work second best. As Western civilization drifted from its Christian roots, its work ethic became decidedly secular and devoid of a religious base. It should be clear, therefore, that a genuinely Christian view of work must be based on something (the Bible) more authoritative and transcendent than mere human thinking, no matter how helpful that thinking is.

To appeal to biblical authority will of course seem like an anomaly in the larger world of modern thought. This leads to a final observation. For the last three centuries, work has been discussed in a nonreligious context, chiefly economic and sociological. A topic that was once regarded as a religious issue has fallen victim to the syndrome of the retreating province of the Christian faith in the modern world. I believe the only hope for work in our day is to return it to the religious arena in which it once took its place, which is the subject of my next chapter.

A HISTORY OF ATTITUDES TOWARD LEISURE

The history of attitudes toward leisure is told more quickly than the history of attitudes toward work. Compared to the ongoing discussion of work, leisure has not received its fair share of attention through the centuries.

The Greek Ideal of Leisure

If the history of work got off to an inauspicious start in classical Greece, the reverse is true for leisure. The Greeks had an exalted view of leisure that remains a standard for today.[27]

Again Aristotle is the leading spokesman. For him, leisure is more than free time, though it requires freedom from the necessity of labor as a prerequisite. Freed *from* the need to work, one was freed *to* engage in the life of contemplation and culture. Leisure was thus a state of being in which an activity was performed for its own sake.

This ideal of leisure was intimately bound up with Greek humanism. Believing in the value of the individual's self-development, the Greeks sought to fulfill the whole person. Leisure was part of this wholeness. It "was a quality of life that enabled man to develop and express all sides of his intellectual, physical and spiritual natures."[28] It is small wonder that this ideal was rooted in the concept of *schole*, from which we get our word *school*. Greek leisure was almost synonymous with liberal education. It fostered contemplation, learning, music, literature, and sports. People were educated for these activities in academies, and facilities for the exercise of these activities from theaters to gymnasiums were also built. We can see, then, why Aristotle contrasted leisure not only to work, but also to children's play, as well as to recreation that simply restores the worker.

Of course this high ideal of cultured leisure carried with it a price tag. It was reserved for a small minority of the population, mainly males of the ruling class. It was, moreover, based on the premise of slave labor.

This brings us to an issue that will run as a unifying theme through any history of leisure. In every era, leisure in its highest reaches has been reserved for a leisured elite. They are the ones who have the education and cultural level to enjoy leisure. It is a privileged state.

This may make it suspect in the eyes of some, but I would suggest a more favorable interpretation. In our own day, when education is universal and where it costs less to read a book than drive a car, we can legitimately speak of the democratization of leisure. It is really within the reach of anyone who values it. Viewed thus, the Greek ideal of leisure as the fully developed person remains a standard for excellence in leisure.

Rome and Mass Leisure

The Romans followed the pattern of the Greeks in planning and building for leisure. For them, too, it remained a goal of civilization to provide meaningful leisure pursuits for its citizens. Rome had its tradition of public leisure, and the monuments to that tradition included baths, theaters, parks, stadiums, and gymnasiums.

As the ruling class became separated from the masses, however, leisure increasingly became a means of entertaining and distracting the potentially revolutionary masses. Leisure thus became "bread and circuses" for the masses. The Greek ideal of the educated and cultured person had degenerated to mere consumption—of public entertainment by the lower classes and of a luxurious lifestyle by the rulers.

Here, then, is an early example of one perversion of leisure: mass consumption of morally degrading or trivial activities. It represents an impulse that always threatens to engulf a society's leisure, and it can be argued that it dominates the leisure scene in our own day.

Medieval Asceticism

The Middle Ages did not produce a lot of theorizing about leisure, but one development is important to my attempt later in this book to integrate leisure with Christianity. I noted in my opening chapter that leisure presupposes the legitimacy of pleasure. The asceticism (denial of pleasure) and otherworldliness of the Catholic Middle Ages carried with it a relatively low regard for leisure. If the main business of life is to avoid earthly pleasure, then leisure will naturally not hold much appeal.

Tertullian's treatise against Roman festivals is one index to this negative attitude.[29] Beginning with the premise, "What greater pleasure is there than distaste of pleasure itself, than contempt of all the world can give?" Tertullian systematically denies the activities of a Roman festival as fit for Christian participation. He asks, "Will the man, seated where there is nothing of God, at that moment think of God?" As for sports, "never can you approve the foolish racing and throwing feats and the more foolish jumping contests; . . . you will hate men bred to amuse the idleness of Greece." All of the arts are condemned on the ground that the demons from the beginning designed them "to turn man from the Lord and bind him to their glorification," giving "inspiration to men of genius in these particular arts."

Augustine came to regard his classical education in similar terms. He believed that "we were forced to go astray in the footsteps of these poetic fictions."[30] He commends Plato for having "absolutely excluded poets from his ideal state."[31] In retrospect, Augustine believed he had "sinned" when, as a schoolboy, he disliked the sound of "one and one, two; two and two, four" but loved to hear "the burning of Troy" and "the wooden horse lined with armed men."[32] We see here a distrust of culture and pleasure, which are viewed as enemies to the Christian life. For Augustine, even eating was sinful if one did it in a spirit of pleasure.[33]

A final example of the negative medieval attitude toward leisure is from a famous letter that the churchman Alcuin wrote in 797. Aware of the monks' fondness for fictional stories about heroes such as Beowulf and Ingeld, Alcuin laid down the rule in a letter to a bishop named Higbald, "Let the words of God be read aloud at table in your refectory. The reader should be heard there, not the flute player; the Fathers of the Church, not the songs of the heathen." To clinch his point, Alcuin asked rhetorically, "What has Ingeld to do with Christ?"[34]

The Catholic Middle Ages did not discredit all leisure. There were many holy days in which common people participated. But we must remember that life in the world had two strikes against it from the beginning. The truly spiritual life was what went on in the monasteries. And what went on there was ascetic and otherworldly, a climate that effectively precluded the practice of leisure as a pleasurable and self-rewarding activity.

The Renaissance and Reformation

The sixteenth and seventeenth centuries present a mixed picture. The rebirth of classical, humanistic values resulted in the greatest flowering of artistic creativity in Western civilization. As in ancient Greece, there was general participation in the arts. To see the attitude of the age, all we need do is look at Renaissance education. It fully embraced culture and the ideal of the educated mind.

Nor should we set these Renaissance humanists up as antagonists of the Puritans. As C. S. Lewis correctly notes, "There was no necessary enmity between Puritans and humanists. They were often the same people, and nearly always the same sort of people."[35]

Yet the ideal of leisure cannot be said to have been very healthy in the Reformation movement. The picture is not as negative as is usually claimed, as I will show in the next chapter. But the Protestant ethic was too utilitarian, too work oriented, and too uptight about the very appearance of evil to allow for a wholehearted endorsement of leisure. Puritans such as Richard Baxter were quick to equate pastimes with timewasting. And even when they affirmed legitimate recreation, the Puritans made it part of their work ethic by defending its usefulness in preparing people to work.

The Triumph of Utilitarianism

The most notable development in attitudes toward leisure between the Reformation and the twentieth century was the growth of utilitarianism.[36] Its chief spokesmen were Jeremy Bentham and John Stuart Mill, but these specific theorists are less important than the general spirit of pragmatism that came to dominate Western culture. Bentham equated happiness with utility, pleasure with profit. "What is the use of it?" was his standard test.

As Mill noted, by the time this equation of happiness and utility became popularized, the word utilitarian came to mean "the rejection, or the neglect . . . of beauty, of ornament, or of amusement." A later spokesman for the position claimed that if a game "be undertaken solely for the sake of the enjoyment attaching to it, we need scarcely take it under our notice," stating additionally that "value depends entirely upon utility."

Of course this utilitarian spirit expressed itself in the industrial society and its accompanying urbanization. Factories and cities followed the course of what was efficient and useful, not what was beautiful and enjoyable and humanly enriching. Such an outlook was on a collision course with leisure, since leisure lies beyond the bounds of what is useful. "In leisure," writes an authority, "man oversteps the frontiers of the everyday, workaday world."[37] Nineteenth-century utilitarianism did what it could to insure that urban workers did not overstep that frontier.

Industrialism changed the social context in which leisure occurred. It made people less the owner of their own time. It speeded up the pace of life, making leisure more necessary but reducing the amount of time available for it. And it created a more distinct cleavage between work and leisure, since work was increasingly undertaken at specific locations and times separate from the rest of life.

The legacy of utilitarianism has been permanent. Individual and communal decisions today tend to be made on the basis of usefulness. It is my observation, moreover, that the test of usefulness is applied with particular rigor by evangelical Christians. The result is a thriving work ethic and an anemic play ethic, along with a virtual neglect of art and culture.

The Twentieth Century: The Age of Leisure

Our own century is surely the age of leisure. Who can doubt it, when several years ago Americans alone spent 262 billion dollars on leisure?[38] This is not to deny the point made earlier that in our fast-paced society people have less leisure than they want or need.

What is new in our century, however, is a widespread acceptance of the legitimacy of leisure and recreation. People do not feel they have to defend sitting down to watch television or visit a park. Leisure has become an expectation of life, a natural right.

The study of leisure has also come into its own in our century. Schools have courses on leisure. Books and articles on the subject multiply each year. In fact, I found many more books and articles on leisure than on work, even though (or perhaps because?) leisure is less understood. Recreation and leisure are also closely tied to public policy today.

Leisure in our century is decidedly pluralistic. Technology has greatly enlarged the range of leisure activities available to us. It has also made the concept of leisure virtually synonymous with mass leisure, with its attendant tendency toward relatively low intellectual and cultural standards.

We should also note that modern leisure exists in a largely secular context. Discussions rarely attempt to place it into a religious frame of reference. Most people in our culture pursue their leisure activities without a thought about the morality of what they are doing or whether it is a good use of time. To put it another way, the constraints on most people's leisure are constraints of time and money, not of religious or moral conscience.

What the History of Attitudes toward Leisure Tells Us

Leisure has fared even worse than work in the history of the human race. In the history of work, we can at least look back to two centuries of the Protestant work ethic for a beacon of Christian understanding. But the Christian understanding of leisure is scarcely a flicker. This means we will get relatively little help from the past in reaching a Christian understanding of leisure.

The main bright spot we can find is the Christian humanism of the Renaissance. It is admirably summarized in the Puritan John Milton's treatise *Of Education*. Milton leaves no doubt that the goal of education is "to know God aright, and out of that knowledge to love him, to imitate him, to be like him." With the Christian context thus established, Milton proceeds to outline his educational ideals. It is an education that is useful for life but also a preparation for leisure.

Milton notes, as Aristotle and Plato had also observed, that the Spartans' educational system equipped their citizens for war but not for peace. Milton accordingly outlines an education that will prepare a person for both work and leisure. A person is expected to enjoy reading, music, and physical exercise. The educational process itself includes times of work, of culture, and of encounters with nature. To transport this breadth of vision into one's leisure time in the twentieth century is not easy. It requires a much higher ideal of leisure than most people today are prepared to accept. But for the Christian, it remains an ideal undergirded with abundant biblical warrant.

FURTHER READING

Adriano Tilgher, *Work: What It Has Meant to Men through the Ages* (1930).
Arthur T. Geoghegan, *The Attitude towards Labor in Early Christianity and Ancient Culture* (1945).
W. R. Forrester, *Christian Vocation* (1953).
Sebastian de Grazia, *Of Time, Work, and Leisure* (1962).
John R. Kelly, *Leisure* (1982).

Chapter 3, Notes

1. In an effort to keep footnotes manageable, let me say that I took all my data regarding classical attitudes toward work from the following sources: Adriano Tilgher, *Work: What It Has Meant to Men through the Ages*, trans. Dorothy C. Fisher (New York: Arno Press, 1930), 3-9; Melvin Kranzberg and Joseph Gies, *By the Sweat of Thy Brow: Work in the Western World* (New York: G. P. Putnam's Sons, 1975), 27-31; Robert L. Heilbroner, *The Making of Economic Society* (Englewood Cliffs, N.J.: Prentice-Hall, 1962), 18-29; and Hannah Arendt, *The Human Condition* (Chicago: University of Chicago Press, 1958), 80-84.

2. Tilgher, 15.

3. Quoted in Joachim Jeremias, *Rediscovering the Parables* (New York: Scribner, 1966), 113.

4. Eusebius, *Demonstratio Evangelica*, as quoted by W. R. Forrester, *Christian Vocation* (New York: Scribner, 1953), 42.

5. Forrester, 45.

6. Tilgher, 35, 38.

7. Ibid., 35-36.

8. Ibid., 39-41.

9. Sebastian de Grazia, *Of Time, Work, and Leisure* (New York: The Twentieth Century Fund, 1962), 30.

10. I have taken all my *Poor Richard* quotations from *Major Writers of America*, ed. Perry Miller (New York: Harcourt, Brace and World, 1962), 1:120-23.

11. William H. Whyte, Jr., *The Organization Man* (New York: Simon and Schuster, 1956), 14-22.

12. Adam Smith, *The Wealth of Nations*, in *Great Books of the Western World*, ed. Robert M. Hutchins (Chicago: Encyclopedia Britannica, 1952), 39:7.

13. John Locke, *The Second Treatise of Civil Government*, chapter 5.

14. Lance Morrow, "What Is the Point of Working?" *Time*, 11 May 1981, 93.

15. For more on the subject, see Robert S. Michaelsen, "Changes in the Puritan Concept of Calling or Vocation," *The New England Quarterly* 26 (1953):315-36; and Paul Marshall, "John Locke: Between God and Mammon," *Canadian Journal of Political Science* 12 (1979):73-96.

16. For an overview of the problems of work in a technological society, one can consult Georges Friedmann, *The Anatomy of Work: Labor, Leisure, and the Implications of Automation*, trans. Wyatt Rawson (Glencoe: Free Press, 1961).

17. Friedrich Engels, *The Condition of the Working Class in England in 1844*, as quoted by Roger Mannell and Seppo Iso-Ahola, "Work Constraints on Leisure: A Social Psychological Analysis," in *Constraints on Leisure*, ed. Michael G. Wade (Springfield, Ill.: Charles C. Thomas, 1985), 157.

18. See *The Marx-Engels Reader*, 2d ed., Robert C. Tucker, ed. (New York: W. W. Norton, 1978).

19. Karl Marx, as quoted by Harold D. Lehman, *In Praise of Leisure* (Scottdale, Penn.: Herald Press, 1974), 82.

20. *Marx-Engels Reader*, 50.

21. Ibid., 64.

22. John Ruskin, excerpts from *The Stones of Venice*, in *The Norton Anthology of English Literature*, ed. M. H. Abrams (New York: W. W. Norton, 1962), 2:1125-29.

23. Excerpts from *Past and Present*, in *English Prose of the Victorian Era*, Charles F. Harrold and William D. Templeman, eds. (New York: Oxford University Press, 1938), 229-33.

24. Robert Dubin, "Industrial Workers' World: A Study of the 'Central Life Interests' of Industrial Workers," in *Work and Leisure: A Contemporary Social Problem*, ed. Erwin O. Smigel (New Haven, Conn.: College and University Press, 1963), 60.

25. Harold L. Wilensky found that "those who have freedom to set their own work schedules tend to choose long hours" ("The Uneven Distribution of Leisure: The Impact of Economic Growth on 'Free Time,'" in *Work and Leisure*, 131).

26. Quoted in Gordon Dahl, *Work, Play, and Worship in a Leisure-Oriented Society* (Minneapolis: Augsburg Publishing House, 1972), 50.

27. I draw my data about classical attitudes toward leisure from these sources: de Grazia, 11-25; John R. Kelly, *Leisure* (Englewood Cliffs, N.J.: Prentice-Hall, 1982), 43-56; and Stanley Parker, *The Sociology of Leisure* (New York: International Publications Service, 1976), 22-23.

28. Kenneth Roberts, *Contemporary Society and the Growth of Leisure* (London: Longman, 1978), 3.q;

29. I have taken all my quotations from Tertullian from *Tertullian: Disciplinary, Moral and Ascetical Works*, trans. Rudolph Arbesmann, in the series entitled *The Fathers of the Church* (New York: Fathers of the Church, 1959), 40:47-107.

30. Augustine, *Confessions*, I, 17.

31. Augustine, *The City of God*, II, 14.

32. *Confessions*, I, 13.

33. Ibid., X, 31.

34. Alcuin, letter to Higbald, is quoted by Eleanor S. Duckett, *Alcuin, Friend of Charlemagne* (New York: Macmillan Publishing Co., 1951), 209.

35. C. S. Lewis, *Studies in Medieval and Renaissance Literature* (Cambridge: Cambridge University Press, 1966), 122.

36. For my sketch of the growth of the utilitarian spirit I have relied on the informal history provided by Walter Kerr, *The Decline of Pleasure* (New York: Simon and Schuster, 1962), 48ff.

37. Josef Pieper, *Leisure the Basis of Culture*, trans. Alexander Dru (New York: Pantheon Books, 1952, 1964), 53.

38. Michael Doan, "$262 Billion Dogfight for Your Leisure Spending," *U.S. News and World Report*, 26 July 1982, 47.

Chapter 4

The Original Protestant Ethic

*I*t is amazing how glibly people speak of "the Puritan ethic," even when they have not read the Puritans. The distortions are not limited to the secular world but have been imported into Christian circles as well. Like Nicodemus, who was a teacher in Israel and yet did not know the basics of the new birth, evangelical Protestants are often strangers to what is best in their own tradition. The purpose of this chapter is to set the record straight regarding the much maligned original Protestants. (For more on the subject than space allows here, I refer readers to my book *Worldly Saints: The Puritans as They Really Were* [Zondervan Publishing House, 1986]).

SIX FALLACIES ABOUT THE PROTESTANT WORK ETHIC

Many of the misconceptions about the original Protestant ethic can be traced to an unjustifiably influential book by Max Weber entitled *The Protestant Ethic and the Spirit of Capitalism* (1930). Believing that the rise of middle class trade occurred chiefly in Protestant countries, Weber argued that there was a connection between "the Protestant ethic" and "the spirit of modern capitalism."

Weber's main thesis, scantily supported with selective quotation from the Puritans, is a classic case of reading back into a movement features that arose two or three centuries later. Scholars have long since shown the inadequacy of Weber's book, showing that instead of the Protestant ethic influencing capitalism, the influence worked the other way—capitalism arose only by changing the original Protestant ethic.[1] Yet Weber's thesis continues to appeal to people who want to blame the ailments of today's work ethic on the Protestant movement. As a way into the subject, therefore, I want to examine six fallacies, six stereotypes of the Protestant ethic that are commonly accepted among those looking for a scapegoat.

Fallacy 1: Work Should Absorb Nearly All One's Time

The common stereotype is that the Protestant ethic led people to devote virtually all of their time to work. One modern writer, for example, describes New England Calvinism as "the tradition that life should be wholly devoted to work."[2]

But the original Protestants preached a clear message of moderation in work. The Puritan divine John Preston wrote, "Take heed of too much business or intending it too much, or inordinately."[3] Richard Steele warned against moonlighting by saying that a person ought not to "accumulate two or three callings merely to increase his riches."[4] Similarly, Martin Luther wrote a letter to Philip Melanchthon in which he told him not to overwork and "then pretend you did it in obedience to God."[5]

The notion that the original Protestants reduced life to continual work is easily refuted by the sheer quantity of time they devoted to spiritual exercises. They set aside Sunday in its entirety for rest from work. They had daily worship in the home and attended midweek meetings. They were also avid readers on religious matters.

Fallacy 2: Self-Interest Is the Motivation for Work

Many of the misleading claims about the Protestant ethic have occurred when people transport modern attitudes toward work onto the original Protestants. An example is the claim that the Reformers taught that people should work hard to get benefits for themselves. At stake here is the question of what constitutes the motivation and reward of work.

Did the original Protestant ethic make a virtue of self-interest? Hardly. Luther wrote that "work should . . . be done to serve God by it, to avoid idleness, and to satisfy His commandments."[6] He also spoke slightingly of people who "do not use their talents in their calling or in the service of their neighbor; they use them only for their own glory and advantage."[7]

Preston said that we must labor "not for our own good, but for the good of others."[8] "Every man for himself, and God for all," wrote William Perkins, "is wicked, and is directly against the end of every calling."[9] And the American Puritan John Cotton wrote that we must "not only aim at our own, but at the public good," with the result that a Christian will not think he has "a comfortable calling, unless it will not only serve his own turn, but the turn of other men."[10]

Fallacy 3: Getting Rich Is the Goal of Life

Though solidly entrenched in the minds of many, the claim that the original Protestants regarded making money as the goal of life is one of the most frivolous of the common charges. The Reformers and Puritans did not despise money and earthly goods, but they emphatically did not regard these as the goal of life.

One of them asserted that "blessedness . . . does not lie in the acquisition of worldly things. Happiness cannot by any art of chemistry be extracted here."[11] Another Puritan told his son, "Travail not too much to be rich. . . . He that is greedy

of gain troubleth his own soul."[12] Richard Baxter believed that
it brings glory to God "when we contemn the riches and honour
of the world," adding that "when seeming Christians are
worldly and ambitious as others, and make as great matter of
the gain and wealth and honour, it showeth that they do but
cover the base and sordid spirit of worldlings with the visor
of the Christian name."[13]

The truth is that the Puritans were obsessed with the
dangers of wealth. William Perkins claimed that "seeking of
abundance is a hazard to the salvation of the soul," elsewhere
commenting, "Let us consider what moved Judas to betray his
master: namely, the desire of wealth."[14] Puritan scholar
Edmund Morgan rightly comments that "the Puritans always
felt more at ease when adversity made them tighten their
belts."[15]

Fallacy 4: People Can Be Successful
through Their Own Efforts

In our own day, the Protestant ethic is described as an
ethic of self-reliance. The Reformers, runs the argument, believed that people can pull themselves up by their own
bootstraps. The harder we work, the more money we will make.
The final result is "the self-made person" our own culture
worships.

The stereotype is exactly wrong so far as the original
Protestants are concerned. The Protestant ethic is an ethic of
grace, not an ethic of merit. In fact, the whole theological bent
of Protestantism opposes the idea of human merit before God.
If salvation is by faith rather than works, how can one earn
one's way?

Calvin thus asserts that "men in vain wear themselves
out with toiling . . . to acquire riches, since these also are a
benefit bestowed only by God."[16] And again, "Whenever we
meet with the word 'reward' or it crosses our minds, let us
realize that it is the height of the divine goodness towards
us."[17] Luther was of the same opinion:

When riches come, the godless heart of man thinks:
I have achieved this with my labors. It does not
consider that these are purely blessings of God,
blessings that at times come to us through our labors
and at times without our labors, but never because
of our labors; for God always gives them because
of His undeserved mercy.[18]

The American Puritan Cotton Mather said aphoristically, "In
our occupation we spread our nets; but it is God who brings
unto our nets all that comes into them."[19]

Fallacy 5: Wealth Is a Sign of God's Favor and Evidence of One's Salvation

Modern scholars often claim that the original Protestants
regarded wealth as a sign of God's favor. But where is the
evidence? I have never seen the claim made by the original
Protestants.

It may come as quite a shock to debunkers to learn that
the original Protestants saw an inverse relationship between
wealth and godliness. Given their position as an often perse-
cuted minority, the early Protestants regarded persecution and
suffering, not earthly success, as the most likely result of godly
living.

The Puritan Thomas Watson claimed that "true godliness
is usually attended with persecution."[20] Baxter warned, "Remember that riches do make it harder for a man to be saved."[21]
Luther called "utterly nonsensical" the "delusion" that led
people to conclude that if someone "has good fortune, wealth,
and health, . . . behold, God is dwelling here."[22] And the
Puritan Samuel Willard wrote, "As riches are not evidences of
God's love, so neither is poverty of his anger or hatred."[23]

Fallacy 6: The Protestant Ethic Approved of All Types of Business Competition

A final fallacy is that the Protestant ethic was the forerun-
ner of modern business practices. In particular, the charge is

made that the Protestant ethic approved of virtually any type of competition and profiteering that led to moneymaking. Once again the modern view strikes out when it confronts what the Reformers and Puritans actually said.

The English Puritan John Knewstub spoke disparagingly of businessmen who "come to buying and selling as it were to the razing and spoiling of some enemy's city . . . where every man catcheth, snatcheth and carrieth away whatsoever he can come by."[24] When Baxter denounced economic abuses, the activities he deemed illegitimate included taking more for goods than they are worth, making a product seem better than it is, concealing flaws in a product, asking as high a price as one thinks he can get, and taking advantage of another person's necessity.[25]

And then there was the celebrated case of Robert Keayne, a merchant of Boston whom the townspeople thought charged excessive prices. Keayne was brought to church trial, fined two hundred pounds by the magistrates, and nearly excommunicated.[26]

Summary

What goes by the name of "the Protestant ethic" today is nearly the opposite of what the original Protestants actually advocated and practiced. Only when the religious conscience and theological framework had been removed did the original Protestant ethic acquire the traits that are mistakenly attributed to it. With the underbrush of modern misconceptions cleared away at least a little, we are ready to explore positively what constituted the original Protestant ethic.

WHAT THE REFORMATION REALLY SAID

The excursion we are about to take into the original Protestant ethic is not a mere historical exercise. In exploring what the Reformation said about work, I am also building the outline for what I believe to be the Christian view of work.

The Virtue of Work

The common stereotype about the Protestant ethic is right in one regard: it *did* assert the value of industrious work. Everywhere we turn in these writers and preachers, we hear a chorus of admonition that God created us to work. We might note in advance that the original Protestants did not advocate work because it was inherently meritorious but because it was God's appointed means of providing for human needs.

To begin, the Protestant tradition made much of work as a creation ordinance, already established by God for the human race before the Fall. Luther noted that "man was created not for leisure but for work, even in the state of innocence."[27] "Adam in his innocence had all things at his will," wrote Perkins, "yet then God employed him in a calling."[28] The effect of viewing work as a creation ordinance and not a result of the Fall was to dignify the very concept of work; work was regarded as a mark of being truly human.

Convinced that work bore God's approval, the Reformers extolled diligence in work. Perkins wrote, "Every man must do the duties of his calling with diligence: and therefore Solomon saith, Ecc. 9:10. Whatsoever is in thine hand to do, do it with all thy power."[29] Not to work diligently is to presume on God's providence. Luther expressed the idea with his usual vividness:

> God does not want to have success come without work . . . . He does not want me to sit at home, to loaf, to commit matters to God, and to wait till a fried chicken flies into my mouth. That would be tempting God.[30]

"God will bless our diligence, not our laziness," said Watson.[31]

Underlying this Protestant affirmation of the need to work is a sturdy realism about what it takes to sustain life in a fallen world. One Puritan wrote, "It is lawful, yea a duty to be diligent in your particular callings; God has commanded us in the sweat of our brows to get our bread."[32] Again, "God hath commanded you some way or another to labour for your daily bread."[33]

The Protestant endorsement of the need to obey God's command to be diligent in our work is well summarized by Robert Bolton's statement that a Christian must

> be diligent with conscience and faithfulness in some lawful, honest particular calling . . . not so much to gather gold . . . as for necessary and moderate provision for family and posterity: and in conscience and obedience to that common charge laid upon all the sons and daughters of Adam to the world's end.[34]

The Protestant Critique of Idleness

Corresponding to the Protestant praise of diligence in work was a steady stream of contempt for idleness and sloth. The social context for this theme was the large number of privileged aristocracy and church-supported clerics that populated Europe at the time of the Reformation.

"God doth allow none to live idly," wrote the English Puritan Arthur Dent in his influential book *The Plain Man's Path- way to Heaven*.[35] His fellow Puritan Robert Bolton called idleness "the very rust and canker of the soul."[36] Baxter agreed: "It is swinish and sinful not to labor."[37]

For the Reformers and Puritans, work was both an individual responsibility and a social obligation. Paul's command that people who do not work should not eat was frequently quoted, as in this statement by Mather: "For those who indulge themselves in idleness, the express command of God unto us is that we should let them starve."[38]

If social privilege was no excuse not to work, neither was "spirituality." Steele spoke against "neglecting man's necessary affairs upon pretense of religious worship."[39] His fellow Puritan Thomas Shepard gave this advice to a religious zealot who complained that spiritual thoughts distracted him while he was at work:

> As it is sin to nourish worldly thoughts when God set you a work in spiritual, heavenly employments,

so it is . . . as great a sin to suffer yourself to be
distracted by spiritual thoughts when God sets you
on work in civil employments.[40]

What emerges from these typical comments is a deeply in-
grained contempt for lazy people.

The Sanctity of All Legitimate Types of Work

Another key element in the Protestant platform was the
sanctity of all legitimate types of work. This conviction began
with a thoroughgoing rejection of the dichotomy between "sacred" and "secular" work. Luther was the person who more
than anyone else overthrew the notion that clergymen, monks,
and nuns were engaged in holier work than the housewife or
shopkeeper. He wrote, "It looks like a small thing when a maid
cooks and cleans and does other housework. But because God's
command is there, even such a small work must be praised as
a service of God far surpassing the holiness and asceticism of
all monks and nuns."[41] Again, household work "has no appearance of sanctity; and yet these very works in connection with
the household are more desirable than all the works of all the
monks and nuns. . . . Seemingly secular works are a worship
of God and an obedience well pleasing to God."[42]

The most important result of this outlook was to sanctify
common work. It opened the door to regarding every task or
job as important in God's eyes. William Tyndale said that if
we look externally "there is difference betwixt washing of
dishes and preaching of the word of God; but as touching to
please God, none at all."[43] According to Perkins, "The action
of a shepherd in keeping sheep . . . is as good a work before
God as is the action of a judge in giving a sentence, or a
magistrate in ruling, or a minister in preaching."[44]

Obviously this view of work renders every task of intrinsic
value and integrates every legitimate vocation with a Christian's
spiritual life. It makes every job consequential by claiming it
as the arena for glorifying God. It provides a way for workers
to serve God not only *within* their work in the world but *through*
that work.

The Protestant Doctrine of Calling or Vocation

With the idea of calling we get to the very heart of the Protestant contribution to ideas about work. Every Christian, said the Reformers, is called by God to serve him. To follow that call is to obey God.

The Reformers actually spoke of a double call by God, and this is important to our understanding of the subject. The general call comes in the same form to every person and consists of the call to conversion and sanctification. In the words of Perkins, "The general calling is the calling of Christianity, which is common to all that live in the church of God. . . . [It] is that whereby a man is called out of the world to be a child of God."[45] Here is the general context within which people perform their work. They are first of all called to be God's people. The Reformers' view of the primacy of the spiritual did not desert them when they came to theorize about work.

The particular calling consists of the specific job and tasks that God places before us in the course of daily living. It focuses on a person's occupation, but it is not limited to that. It includes one's work more generally. As Gustaf Wingren puts it in his book *Luther on Vocation*, "The life of the home, the relation between parents and children, is vocation, even as is life in the field of labor. . . . From this it is clear that every Christian occupies a multitude of offices at the same time, not just one. . . . All these are vocations."[46] Perkins described vocation as "a certain kind of life, ordained and imposed on man by God, for the common good."[47]

Several important corollaries follow from the Protestant doctrine of vocation. Since God is the one who calls people to their work, the worker becomes a steward who serves God. Work ceases to be viewed only in itself and instead becomes an act of obedience and service to God. "Whatsoever our callings be," wrote a Puritan, "we serve the Lord Jesus Christ in them."[48] To perform one's tasks, in this view, is to work in the sight of God.

Another practical result of the doctrine of Christian calling is that it leads to contentment in one's work. If one's work comes from God, one has a reason to accept the work. Luther wrote, "Nothing is so bad . . . but what it becomes sweet and tolerable if only I know and am certain that it is pleasing to God."[49] Calvin was of a similar opinion:

> In all our cares, toils, annoyances, and other burdens, it will be no small alleviation to know that all these are under the superintendence of God. . . . This, too, will afford admirable consolation in following your proper calling. No work will be so mean and sordid as not to have a splendor and value in the eye of God.[50]

I will return to the doctrine of calling later in this book. In the original Protestant ethic, it combined a cluster of related ideas: the providence of God in arranging human work, work as the response of a steward to God, and contentment with one's tasks. Cotton's advice about work sums it up: "Serve God in thy calling, and do it with cheerfulness, and faithfulness, and an heavenly mind."[51]

Work as Service to God and Society

A main emphasis of the original Protestant ethic was to delineate the motivations and rewards of work. The rewards of work were overwhelmingly conceived as spiritual and moral. Work glorified God and benefited society. Perkins sounded the keynote:

> The main end of our lives . . . is to serve God in the serving of men in the works of our callings. . . . Some man will say perchance: What, must we not labor in our callings to maintain our families? I answer: this must be done: but this is not the scope and end of our lives. The true end of our lives is to do service to God in serving of man.[52]

According to Baxter, the purpose of work is "obeying God and doing good to others."[53] And Steele advised, "Direct all to . . . the honour of God, the public good as well as your private commodity. . . . You are working for God."[54]

Although the Reformers and Puritans generally believed that one should remain loyal to one's calling and avoid casual changes in occupation, it is untrue that they uncritically accepted the vocational structure as it existed in their day.[55] Virtually every Protestant writer on the subject spoke of "lawful" or "warrantable" or "honest" callings, implying that some occupations did not measure up to such a standard of Christian morality. The original Protestant's grip on the moral and spiritual goals of work provided a standard by which to judge the choice of a vocation. William Ames wrote,

> It is not enough that one should simply work: He must work for what is good, Eph. 4:28. Quietly and diligently let him follow an occupation which agrees with the will of God and the profit of men, 1 Thess. 4:11, 12; 2 Thess. 3:12.[56]

A group of Puritan ministers meeting in Boston in 1699 agreed that no occupation "is lawful but what is useful unto human society."[57]

In a similar vein, Baxter urged,

> Choose that employment or calling in which you may be most serviceable to God. Choose not that in which you may be most rich or honorable in the world; but that in which you may do most good, and best escape sinning.[58]

If "two callings equally conduce to the public good," added Baxter, "and one of them hath the advantage of riches and the other is more advantageous to your souls, the latter must be preferred."[59] We can see, then, that the Protestant emphasis on the moral and spiritual ends of work was not merely idealistic theory. It had a practical influence on how people viewed their work.

Moderation in Work

In addition to providing a balanced Christian view of the goal and rewards of work, the Protestant work ethic aimed at an ideal of moderation in work. Moderation involves a golden mean between opposite extremes. This is what the Protestant ethic proclaimed in theory.

On the one side, the Protestant ethic avoided idleness and laziness. "Certainly God curses laziness and loafing," said Calvin, who went on to denounce "idlers and good-for-nothing individuals who live by the sweat of others."[60] Two "damnable sins" that Perkins rebuked were "idleness, whereby the duties of our callings . . . are neglected or omitted," and "slothfulness, whereby they are performed slackly and carelessly."[61]

The other extreme that the Protestant ethic condemned was excessive devotion to work and wealth. The English Puritan Philip Stubbes wrote, "So far from covetousness and from immoderate care would the Lord have us that we ought not this day to care for tomorrow, for (saith he) sufficient to the day is the travail of the same."[62] Cotton urged moderation in work with the statement that although the Christian must "labor most diligently in his calling, yet his heart is not set upon these things."[63]

Since attitudes toward work and wealth are so closely intertwined, we might note that the Protestant affirmation of moderation extended to possessions as well as work. Perkins denounced "excessive seeking of worldly wealth, when men keep no measure or moderation."[64] His fellow Puritan Cotton Mather spoke out against people's "insatiable desire after land and worldly accommodations . . . only so that they might have elbow room in the world."[65]

It is in this context of setting boundaries to work that we can understand Protestant Sabbatarianism, which was especially important to the English Puritans. For them, Sunday observance was part of social action. This explains why not all Sabbatarians were Puritans. The reason national and local governments of the time were so zealous in passing and enforcing Sabbath laws was that without it some employers would have forced people to work seven days a week.

Sunday observance protected workers who (in Baxter's words) "would be left remediless under such masters as would both oppress them with labour, and restrain them from God's service."[66] Arthur Hildersham said that Sunday observance was especially necessary for hardworking people who were in danger of having their hearts "corrupted and glued to the world."[67] A modern authority on the Puritans claims that "in the seventeenth century there was only one way in which the industrious sort could be protected from themselves: by the total prohibition of Sunday work."[68]

Summary

The Protestant work ethic, rightly so-called, is almost the opposite of what people today take it to mean. Starting from the assumption that work is a virtue and idleness a vice, the original Protestants asserted the sanctity of all legitimate types of work, viewing them as the response of a steward to a call from God. Service to God and society was viewed as the ultimate goal of work, which was to be undertaken with a sense of moderation. These ideas about work are not simply specimens in a historical museum; they remain a standard to guide Christian thought on work today.

DID THE PURITANS OUTLAW FUN?
EXAMINING SOME COMMON CHARGES

The Protestant movement has been even more ridiculed and misrepresented for its attitude toward leisure than for its ideas about work. The Puritans have taken the brunt of the attack, and I will accordingly speak of "the Puritans" in the remainder of this chapter. We will begin by assessing the accuracy or inaccuracy of some common charges.

Charge 1: The Puritans Were Opposed to Fun

Untrue. Against a modern debunker's view that Puritanism "damages the human soul, renders it hard and gloomy, deprives it of sunshine and happiness,"[69] we may place statements such as these by the Puritans themselves: "God would have our joys to be far more than our sorrows";[70] Christians "may be merry at their work, and merry at their meat."[71] Thomas Gataker wrote that it is the purpose of Satan to persuade us that "in the kingdom of God there is nothing but sighing and groaning and fasting and prayer," whereas the truth is that "in his house there is marrying and giving in marriage . . . feasting and rejoicing."[72]

Charge 2: The Puritans Did Not Allow Sports or Recreation

Largely false. The more that recent scholarship has learned about the Puritans, the more questionable older views of their hostility to recreation have become. The best source of information is Hans-Peter Wagner's book-length study entitled *Puritan Attitudes Towards Recreation in Early Seventeenth Century America.*[73] It shows that the Puritans enjoyed such varied sports as hunting, fishing, bowling, reading, music, swimming, skating, and archery. A Puritan preacher said regarding recreations that Christians should "enjoy them as liberties, with thankfulness to God that allows us these liberties to refresh ourselves."[74] Another wrote that

> God has . . . adjudged some diversion or recreation . . . to be both needful and expedient. . . . A wise and good man . . . is forced to . . . let religion choose such recreations as are healthful, short, recreative, and proper, to refresh both mind and body.[75]

Cotton Mather preached a sermon in which he gave his parishioners advice about "how to employ the leisure of the winter for the glory of God."[76] Most important of all, a parliamentary act of 1647, when the Puritans controlled Parliament, decreed that every second Tuesday of the month was to be a holiday when all shops, warehouses, and places of business were to be closed from eight in the morning until eight in the evening for the recreation of the workers.[77]

Charge 3: The Puritans Passed Laws Prohibiting Some Forms of Recreation

Yes they did, but this does not represent opposition to recreation in principle. This modern stereotype of the Puritans is based on a misreading of the evidence. The Puritans rejected all sports on Sundays and selected sports at all times. Their rejection of sports on Sunday was based on their view that the entire day was to be devoted to spiritual activities, chiefly worship and rest from the ordinary concerns of the week.

The Puritans rejected other sports on moral grounds. These included games of chance, gambling, bear baiting, horse racing, and bowling in or around taverns. By modern standards, some of their prohibitions seem frivolous, such as their outlawing the game of shuffleboard.[78] If there is any defense of the Puritans on these matters it is that small details can signal larger issues when we consider a total lifestyle. In particular, the Puritans were uptight about games, idleness, and carousing that occurred in or around taverns.

Charge 4: The Puritans Abolished Many of the Holidays that Had Prevailed in the Middle Ages

True. Under medieval Catholicism, the number of holy days grew to as many as 115 days per year, not counting Sundays.[79] The Puritans rejected such days on religious grounds, and whatever leisure elements they contained went as well. We should remember that social conditions were changing and that society was becoming less and less rural, so that the loss of church holidays would have occurred for economic reasons quite apart from the Puritan movement.

What the critics fail to tell us is that the Puritans had their own religious activities that in many ways took the place of the Catholic holy days. One was the rigorous keeping of Sunday as a day of rest and worship. Then, too, the Puritans loved visiting and feasts. The idea of celebrating the American

Thanksgiving Day was vintage Puritanism, and we might note
that the original thanksgiving celebration lasted at least three
days.[80]

The Puritans, in fact, made a regular practice of calling
their own family days of thanksgiving, to which they usually
invited friends and neighbors. Here is how a specimen entry
in a Puritan diary records such an event:

> We had a solemn day of thanksgiving at my house
> for my wife's and son's recovery; my son Eliezer
> began, Mr. Dawson, John proceeded, I concluded
> with preaching, prayer; we feasted 50 persons and
> upwards, blessed be God.[81]

A Puritan minister's diary indicates that he attended anywhere
from forty-seven to sixty-four such days of thanksgiving in a
typical year.[82]

We should also note that Puritan New England celebrated
events that have dropped out of the annual calendar. Days of
festivity were set aside for ordinations of ministers, lecture
days, election days, training days, commencement days for
courts, and graduation days for college.[83] Wedding celebrations
were yet another occasion for holidays.

Charge 5: The Puritans Had a Negative
Attitude toward Culture and the Arts

Only partly true. Their bad reputation rests partly on a
misreading of the evidence. For example, it is well-known that
the Puritans removed art and organs from the churches. But
this was an objection to Catholic worship and ceremony, not
to music and art themselves.[84] In fact, after removing organs
and paintings from churches, the Puritans often bought them
for private use in their homes.[85] John Cotton wrote a treatise
stating the usual objections to musical instruments in church,
but he went on to say that he did not "forbid the private use
of any instrument of music."[86]

Oliver Cromwell removed an organ from an Oxford chapel
to his own residence at Hampton Court, where he employed

a private organist. When one of his daughters was married, Cromwell engaged an orchestra of forty-eight to accompany the dancing.[87] While confined to prison, John Bunyan not only wrote fictional stories but secretly made a flute out of a chair leg.

On the negative side, although the Puritans fostered religious literature, they had a distressingly hostile view of other forms of literature.[88] It is to their discredit that they closed the theaters at a time when Shakespeare was common fare, though even here we should remember that the objections were partly political and moral, not necessarily extending to the act of reading plays. It is also necessary to make a distinction between "low-brow" Puritans and educated Puritans. The latter were thoroughly saturated in classical literature and were, in fact, the earliest translators of the classics into English.[89]

Charge 6: The Puritans Took the Color Out of Life by Wearing Drab, Unfashionable Clothes

Untrue. The Puritans dressed according to the fashions of their class and time. It is true that black carried connotations of dignity and formality (as it does today) and was standard for clothes worn on Sundays and special occasions.

The Quaker George Fox, a contemporary of the Puritans, paints quite a different picture of them than modern people have. Fox writes slightingly of their "ribbons and lace and costly apparel," as well as their "sporting and feasting."[90] Surviving inventories of clothes show the popularity of russet, various shades of orange-brown, red, blue, green, yellow, and purple.[91]

Summary

Most of the modern charges against the Puritans are either untrue or exaggerated. They tend to be based on the Puritans' bias against selected *manifestations* of leisure activities that were acceptable to the Puritans *in principle*. Within their religious and moral framework, the Puritans engaged in a healthy range of leisure activities.

PURITAN CONTRIBUTIONS TO LEISURE

Out of the mixture of good and bad attitudes toward leisure that we find among the Puritans, it is not hard to extract the positive contributions they made. These, in turn, will make a reappearance when we consider a Christian view of leisure for today.

Religious Activities as Part of Leisure

I am not at all certain that the Puritans would have approved of putting religious activities under the heading of leisure. But there is a sense in which they put religious activities in the place where others had put ordinary recreations.

In the opening chapter we defined leisure partly in terms of its ability to refresh, to provide a break from the everyday routine, to draw a boundary around the acquisitive aspects of life. By such standards, many of the Puritans' religious activities and exercises infused an element of godly leisure into their lives.

I think, for example, of their prizing of "Christian conference," by which they meant conversations with Christians of like mind that left the conversers refreshed. John Winthrop records in his diary a "conference with a Christian friend or two," adding that "God so blessed it unto us, as we were all much quickened and refreshed by it."[92] An extension of this desire for social interaction was the Puritans' love of dinners and social meals.

The Puritan Sabbath also had a dimension of leisure to it. It set a limit to the acquisitive urge. In fact, Ames used this to distinguish between proper and improper Sunday activities. Inappropriate activities were "those which concern our wealth and profit."[93] Nicholas Bownde similarly argued that we cannot attend to God's business if we are encumbered with worldly business on Sunday.[94]

Refusal to Exempt Leisure from Spiritual and Moral Standards

A second great strength of the Puritans was their refusal to exempt leisure from spiritual and moral considerations. The discussion and practice of leisure in our own century is conducted by most people in an amoral atmosphere in which religious implications are considered irrelevant. This secular spirit has invaded the practice of leisure by many Christians as well.

The Puritans stand as a corrective. They expected leisure pursuits to measure up to the criterion of being "lawful." Perkins, for example, listed four religious and moral principles by which to judge leisure: (1) recreations must be "of the best report"; (2) they "must be profitable to ourselves and others, and they must tend to the glory of God"; (3) their purpose "must be to refresh our bodies and minds"; and (4) their use "must be moderate and sparing" of time and "affections."[95] There is something potentially legalistic about such a list, but its virtue is that it applies religious standards to leisure pursuits.

The same concern for morality in leisure underlies some of the Puritan prohibitions of selected recreations. They objected to bear baiting and cock fighting, for example, as being cruel to animals and violent for people. They disliked sports at taverns because of the drunkenness and low moral standards that usually prevailed at such places. They objected to plays and fictional romances because of the immoral behavior portrayed in some of them. Even when I disagree with where the Puritans drew the line, I admire them for applying Christian moral standards to leisure activities.

Moderation in Leisure

While affirming leisure itself, the Puritans were aware that it could be pursued in excess. It could, for example, take too much of a person's time, as Increase Mather noted: "For a Christian to use recreations is very lawful, and in some cases a great duty, but to waste so much time in any recreation . . . as gamesters usually do at cards and dice, and tables, is heinously sinful."[96] Cotton Mather similarly preached that "moderate recreations . . . are more than a little healthful and useful," but he went on to warn that

> the most harmless recreations may become very culpable and hurtful for want of observing proper rules with regard to time, place, company, manner. . . . God expects that in everything you . . . act under the governance of reason and virtue, and accordingly that you . . . be always sparing of [diversions], that you time them well, regulate them prudently, make them give place to business, make them subserve religion.[97]

The Puritans urged moderation not only in the time devoted to recreation but also the money spent on it.[98]

The Ideal of Christian Culture

The stereotype of the Puritans as uneducated and uncultured people is exactly wrong. They were highly educated. Their education, moreover, gave them an acquaintance with classical culture. At their best, the Puritans valued what I will call Christian culture, by which I include culture that by God's common grace expresses truth and beauty even when produced by non-Christians.

There is evidence that the Puritans favored intellectual and cultural leisure pursuits over physical recreation.[99] The Puritans were great readers, for example. The study of literature in the schools can be traced back to Puritan schools.[100] Puritan writers of imaginative literature include such giants as Edmund Spenser, John Milton, and John Bunyan. Music was equally valued by educated Puritans, as Percy Scholes' book *Music in Puritan England and New England* abundantly shows.

The home in which John Milton was raised illustrates the Puritan ideal of Christian culture. Milton's father, who had been put out of his parental home and permanently disinherited when his Catholic father found him reading an English Bible in his room, was sufficiently accomplished at music to have several of his compositions published. There was an organ in the home. Milton himself was thoroughly acquainted with music and literature during his years at home and college. With the advantage of an upbringing like this, it is perhaps no surprise that Milton could write later in life that "we . . . have need of some delightful intermissions, wherein the enlarged soul . . . may keep her holidays to joy and harmless pastime."[101]

WHERE THE PURITANS FAILED IN REGARD TO LEISURE

Despite much that is positive about the Puritans' attitude toward leisure, the overall picture remains unsatisfactory. Three main failings can be discerned.

A Legalistic Approach to Leisure

The first thing to make us uneasy about the Puritan attitude toward leisure is the number of rules with which they surrounded leisure activities. As already noted, the Puritans expected leisure activities to measure up to moral and spiritual standards. But the number of such standards was sometimes so great that the effect was to undermine the Puritans' theoretic endorsement of leisure.

Baxter, for example, devised a list of eighteen qualifications that governed a Christian's choice of leisure.[102] It must be for the ends of serving God and helping us "in our ordinary callings and duty." Recreation must not be profane or obscene, and it must not harm others. Sports are unlawful that "occasion the multiplying of idle words about them." Furthermore, if a person chooses a "less fit and profitable" leisure pursuit "when a better might be chosen, it is . . . sin." The net result of such stipulations is to instill an aura of suspicion about leisure, even though theoretically it is "lawful."

Being Uptight about Leisure

The number of rules with which the Puritans circumscribed leisure suggests a related problem. They were simply too uneasy about it. They frequently conveyed the impression of "looking for trouble" when they considered the leisure activities people pursued in their society.

The closing of the theaters is an example. Puritan objections to attending plays encompassed a wide range of arguments that are notably lacking in substance. They included claims like these: theaters contributed to the spread of plagues; there was danger that the scaffolding of the playhouses might collapse; male actors wore women's clothing and impersonated female characters; attending plays competed with church attendance; it is hypocritical for players to act a role other than their real-life identity; plays appeal to the most sensual people and are repugnant to the "best and wisest persons"; plays were of pagan origin; plays are not associated with godly persons in the Bible; plays have harmed "thousands of young people"; and on and on. The truth is, I believe, that the Puritans were simply uneasy about attendance at theaters. It did not quite fit their lifestyle. They were therefore quick to latch onto any argument that surfaced against attendance at theaters.

The same Puritan uneasiness about recreation is evident in other leisure activities they prohibited. A New England law, for example, ordered constables to "search after all manner of gaming, singing and dancing" and to report "disordered meetings" even when they occurred in private homes.[103] In Boston a request for an exhibition of tightrope walking was rejected "lest the said divertisement may tend to promote idleness in the town and great mispense of time."[104] This is similar in tone to a Connecticut law that prohibited "the game called shuffle board . . . whereby much precious time is spent unfruitfully."[105] The general tenor of such Puritan pronouncements is a quickness to think the worst of leisure and to ban an activity that carried either the appearance or potential for abuse.

A Utilitarian Attitude toward Leisure

As we have seen, the Puritans were not opposed to leisure in principle. But their defense of leisure was essentially a utilitarian defense. Leisure was good because it made work possible. It was not something valued for its own sake, or as a celebration of life, or as an enlargement of the human spirit.

One Puritan wrote, for example, that "recreation belongs not to rest, but to labor; and it is used that men may by it be made more fit to labor."[106] Recreation "serveth only to make us more able to continue in labour," wrote another.[107]

This utilitarian leisure ethic was a result of the Puritans' overemphasis on work. If work is the best use of time, then leisure becomes a frivolous use of time. Baxter equated "pastimes" with "time wasting" and rejected the very word as "infamous."[108] He therefore advised,

> Keep up a high esteem of time and be every day more careful that you lose none of your time. . . . And if vain recreation, dressings, feastings, idle talk, unprofitable company, or sleep be any of them temptations to rob you of any of your time, accordingly heighten your watchfulness.[109]

If all of one's time is to be devoted to something useful, leisure will obviously fare poorly. This is often what happened in the utilitarian ethic of the Puritans.

Summary

Although the Puritans did not reject leisure in theory, and although they enjoyed many leisure pursuits (especially the more intellectual types such as reading), their practice often reflected a distrust of leisure. Their multiplication of rules showed their uneasiness about leisure, and they made their leisure ethic an appendage to their work ethic.

FURTHER READING

R. H. Tawney, *Religion and the Rise of Capitalism* (1926).
Percy Scholes, *The Puritans and Music in England and New England* (1934).
Robert S. Michaelsen, "Changes in the Puritan Concept of Calling or Vocation," *New England Quarterly* 26 (1953):315-36.

Christopher Hill, *Society and Puritanism in Pre-Revolutionary England* (1964).

Hans-Peter Wagner, *Puritan Attitudes towards Recreation in Early Seventeenth-Century New England* (1982).

Leland Ryken, *Worldly Saints: The Puritans as They Really Were* (1986).

Chapter 4, Notes

1. Sources that show the inadequacy of the Weber thesis include these: Albert Hyma, *Christianity, Capitalism and Communism: A Historical Analysis* (Ann Arbor: George Wahr, 1937); A. M. Robertson, *Aspects of the Rise of Economic Individualism* (New York: Kelley and Millman, 1959); W. R. Forrester, *Christian Vocation* (New York: Charles Scribner's Sons, 1953), 152-67; Robert W. Green, ed., *Protestantism and Capitalism: The Weber Thesis and Its Critics* (Boston: D. C. Heath, 1959); and Michael Walzer, *The Revolution of the Saints: A Study in the Origins of Radical Politics* (Cambridge: Harvard University Press, 1965).

2. Max Kaplan, *Leisure in America: A Social Inquiry* (New York: John Wiley and Sons, 1960), 151.

3. John Preston, *The Saint's Qualification*, as quoted in Charles H. George and Katherine George, *The Protestant Mind of the English Reformation, 1570-1640* (Princeton: Princeton University Press, 1961), 172.

4. Richard Steele, *The Tradesman's Calling*, as quoted by R. H. Tawney, *Religion and the Rise of Capitalism* (New York: Harcourt, Brace, 1926), 244.

5. Martin Luther, letter to Melanchthon, as printed in Ewald M. Plass, ed., *What Luther Says: An Anthology* (St. Louis: Concordia Publishing House, 1959), 787.

6. Luther, sermon on the fourth petition of the Lord's Prayer, as printed in Plass, 1494.

7. Luther, sermon in 1 Peter 4:8-11, in Plass, 1497.

8. John Preston, *The New Covenant*, as quoted in George, 137.

9. William Perkins, *A Treatise of the Vocations or Callings of Men*, in *Puritan Political Ideas, 1558-1794*, ed. Edmund S. Morgan (Indianapolis: Bobbs-Merrill, 1965), 56.

10. John Cotton, *Christian Calling*, in *The Puritans*, rev. ed., edited by Perry Miller and Thomas H. Johnson (New York: Harper and Row, 1963), 1:320.

11. Thomas Watson, *The Beatitudes* (Edinburgh: Banner of Truth Trust, 1977), 25.

12. Lord Montagu, as quoted by Lawrence Stone, *The Crisis of the Aristocracy, 1558-1641* (Oxford: Oxford University Press, 1965), 331.

13. Richard Baxter, *A Christian Directory*, as excerpted in *Capitalism and the Reformation*, ed. M. J. Kitch (London: Longmans, Green, 1967), 156-57.

14. William Perkins, *Works*, as excerpted in Kitch, 108; and quoted in George, 172.

15. Edmund Morgan, "The Puritan Ethic and the American Revolution," in *Puritanism and the American Experience*, ed. Michael McGiffert (Reading, Mass.: Addison-Wesley, 1969), 185.

16. Calvin, commentary on Psalm 127:2, in *Commentary on the Book of Psalms*, trans. James Anderson (Grand Rapids, Mich.: Wm. B. Eerdmans Publishing Co., 1949), 5:107.

17. Calvin, commentary on Luke 17:7, in *A Harmony of the Gospels Matthew, Mark and Luke*, trans. T. H. L. Parker (Grand Rapids, Mich.: Wm. B. Eerdmans Publishing Co., 1972), 2:124.

18. Luther, exposition of Deuteronomy 8:17-18, in Plass, 1495.

19. Cotton Mather, *Sober Sentiments*, as quoted by Ralph Barton Perry, *Puritanism and Democracy* (New York: Vanguard, 1944), 312.

20. Watson, 259.

21. Baxter, *Christian Directory*, as quoted by Hyma, 224.

22. Luther, exposition on Genesis 19:2-3, in Plass, 1436.

23. Samuel Willard, *A Complete Body of Divinity*, as quoted by Stephen Foster, *Their Solitary Way: The Puritan Social Ethic in the First Century of Settlement in New England* (New Haven, Conn.: Yale University Press, 1971), 128.

24. John Knewstub, *Ninth Lecture on the Twentieth Chapter of Exodus*, in *Elizabethan Puritanism*, ed. Leonard J. Trinterud (New York: Oxford University Press, 1971), 351.

25. Baxter, *Chapters from A Christian Directory*, ed. Jeannette Tawney (London: G. Bell and Sons, 1925), 102-12.

26. John Winthrop's *Journal* contains the account; see McGiffert, 115-16.

27. Luther, exposition on Genesis 2:14, in Plass, 1494.

28. Perkins, *Works*, as quoted in George, 132.

29. Perkins, *A Treatise of the Vocations or Callings of Men*, in *Puritan Political Ideas*, ed. Morgan, 42.

30. Luther, exposition on Exodus 13:18, in Plass, 1496.

31. Watson, 257.

32. Joshua Moody, *A Practical Discourse Concerning the Choice Benefit of Communion with God*, as quoted by Emory Elliott, *Power and the Pulpit in Puritan New England* (Princeton: Princeton University Press, 1975), 180-81.

33. Baxter, *Christian Directory*, in Kitch, 156.

34. Robert Bolton, *Works*, as quoted by Horton Davies, *Worship and Theology in England: From Cranmer to Hooker, 1534-1603* (Princeton: Princeton University Press, 1970), 65-66.

35. Arthur Dent, *The Plain Man's Path-way to Heaven*, as quoted in Christopher Hill, *Society and Puritanism in Pre-Revolutionary England* (New York: Schocken Books, 1964), 139.

36. Bolton, as quoted in George, 130.

37. Baxter, *The Catechizing of Families*, as quoted by Hill, 139.

38. Mather, *Durable Riches*, as quoted by Hill, 286.

39. Steele, quoted by R. H. Tawney, 245.

40. Thomas Shepard, as quoted by Perry Miller, *The New England Mind: The Seventeenth Century* (Cambridge: Harvard University Press, 1939), 44.

41. Luther, *Works*, as quoted by Forrester, 148.

42. Luther, commentary on Genesis 13:13.

43. William Tyndale, *The Parable of the Wicked Mammon*, as quoted by Louis B. Wright, *Middle-Class Culture in Elizabethan England* (Chapel Hill: University of North Carolina Press, 1935), 171.

44. Perkins, *Works*, as quoted by Davies, 66.

45. Perkins, *Callings of Men*, in Morgan, 43-44.

46. Gustaf Wingren, *Luther on Vocation*, trans. Carl C. Rasmussen (Philadelphia: Muhlenberg Press, 1957), 5.

47. Perkins, *Callings of Men*, as quoted by Hill, 136.

48. John Dod and Robert Cleaver, *Ten Sermons* . . ., quoted by Davies, 66.

49. Luther, *The Estate of Marriage*, in *Luther's Works*, ed. Jaroslav Pelikan and Helmut T. Lehmann (St. Louis: Concordia Publishing House, 1962), 45:49.

50. Calvin, *Institutes of the Christian Religion*, 3. 10. 6, trans. Henry Beveridge (Grand Rapids, Mich.: Wm. B. Eerdmans Publishing Co., 1972), 2:35.

51. Cotton, in Miller and Johnson, 1:326.

52. Perkins, *Callings of Men*, in Morgan, 56-57.

53. Baxter, *Christian Directory*, as quoted by Perry, 307.

54. Steele, in Kitch, 115.

55. The charge is made by Paul Marshall "Vocation, Work and Jobs," in *Labour of Love: Essays on Work*, Josina Zylstra, ed. (Toronto: Wedge, 1980), 12-14. On the contrary, Baxter wrote that "the first and principal thing to be intended in the choice of a trade or calling for yourselves or children is the service of God and the public good. . . . Some callings are employed about matters of so little use . . . that he that may choose better should be loathe to take up with one of these, though possibly in itself it may be lawful" (*Christian Directory*, in Kitch, 157). Calvin's commentary on 1 Corinthians 7:20 explains what he meant by his cautions against easily leaving one's occupation for another: the apostle Paul, writes Calvin, "only wishes to correct the thoughtless eagerness which impels some to change their situation without any proper reason. . . . He does not lay it down that each person must remain in a certain way of life, once he has adopted it; but, on the other hand, he condemns the restlessness which prevents individuals from remaining contentedly as they are." Cotton Mather wrote, "When a man is become unfit for his business, or his business becomes unfit for him, unquestionably he may leave it; and a man may be otherwise invited sometimes justly to change his business. . . . But many a man, merely from covetousness and from discontent throws up his business" (*A Christian at His Calling*, in McGiffert, 127).

56. William Ames, *The Marrow of Theology*, ed. John D. Eusden (Boston: Pilgrim, 1968), 322.

57. Mather, *Magnalia Christi Americana*, as quoted by Edmund S. Morgan, *The Puritan Family: Religion and Domestic Relations in Seventeenth Century New England* (New York: Harper and Row, 1966), 71.

58. Baxter, *Christian Directory*, in Green, 72.

59. Ibid., 60.

60. Calvin, as quoted by Andre Bieler, *The Social Humanism of Calvin*, trans. Paul T. Fuhrmann (Richmond: John Knox Press, 1961), 45.

61. Perkins, *Callings of Men*, in Morgan, 42-43.

62. Philip Stubbes, *The Anatomy of the Abuses in England*, as quoted by Tawney, *Rise of Capitalism* , 216.

63. Cotton, as quoted by Perry Miller, 42.

64. Perkins, *Works*, in Kitch, 109.

65. Mather, *Magnalia*, as quoted by Hyma, 250.

66. Baxter, *Catechizing of Families*, as quoted in Hill, 166.

67. Arthur Hildersham, *CLII Lectures Upon Psalm LI*, as quoted by Hill, 175.

68. Hill, 152.

69. Langdon Mitchell, as quoted by Perry, 240.

70. Baxter, *The Saints' Everlasting Rest* (Westwood, N.J.: Fleming H. Revell, 1962), 182.

71. Richard Rogers, *Seven Treatises*, as quoted in Irvonwy Morgan, *The Godly Preachers of the Elizabethan Church* (London: Epworth, 1965), 143.

72. Thomas Gataker, *A Wife Indeed*, as quoted in Laurence Lerner, *Love and Marriage: Literature and Its Social Context* (New York: St. Martin's Press, 1979), 112.

73. Hans-Peter Wagner, *Puritan Attitudes Towards Recreation in Early Seventeenth-Century America* (Frankfurt: Verlag Peter Lang, 1982).

74. Richard Sibbes, *Works*, as quoted in Foster, 106.

75. William Burkitt, *The Poor Man's Help*, as quoted in Wagner, 46.

76. Wagner, 14.

77. Percy Scholes, *The Puritans and Music in England and New England* (London: Oxford University Press, 1934), 110-11.

78. Kaplan, 151.

79. John R. Kelly, *Leisure* (Englewood Cliffs, N.J.: Prentice-Hall, 1982), 57.

80. Wagner, 14.

81. Oliver Heywood, *Diary*, as quoted in Horton Davies, *The Worship of the English Puritans* (Westminster: Dacre, 1948), 282.

82. Ibid., 283.

83. Wagner, 18.

84. The best source to consult on this subject is Percy Scholes, *Puritans and Music*. For a bibliography of further sources, see footnote 5 on p. 261 of my book *Worldly Saints: The Puritans as They Really Were* (Grand Rapids,

Mich.: Zondervan Publishing House, 1986).

85. Scholes, 6.

86. Ibid., 5.

87. Ibid.

88. For more on negative Puritan attitudes toward literature, see Lawrence A. Sasek, *The Literary Temper of the English Puritans* (New York: Greenwood, 1961); and Russell Fraser, *The War Against Poetry* (Princeton: Princeton University Press, 1970).

89. See C. H. Conley, *The First English Translators of the Classics* (New Haven, Conn.: Yale University Press, 1927).

90. George Fox, *Journal* (London: J. M. Dent and Sons, 1924), 151.

91. John Demos, *A Little Commonwealth: Family Life in Plymouth Colony* (New York: Oxford University Press, 1970), 53-54.

92. Winthrop, *Winthrop Papers*, as quoted in J. Sears McGee, *The Godly Man in Stuart England: Anglicans, Puritans, and the Two Tables, 1620-1670* (New Haven, Conn.: Yale University Press, 1976), 196.

93. Ames, *Marrow of Theology*, 299.

94. Nicholas Bownde, *The Doctrine of the Sabbath*, as quoted in James T. Dennison, *The Market Day of the Soul: The Puritan Doctrine of the Sabbath in England, 1532-1700* (Lanthan, N.Y.: University Press of America, 1983), 39.

95. Perkins, *Cases of Conscience*, as cited by Sasek, 114.

96. Increase Mather, *Testimony against Several Profane and Superstitious Customs*, in Wagner, 61.

97. Cotton Mather, *Winter-Meditations*, in Wagner, 61.

98. Baxter, *Christian Directory*, cited by Wagner, 51.

99. See Wagner, 86-94, and Scholes.

100. See Roland Frye, *Perspective on Man: Literature and the Christian Tradition* (Philadelphia: Westminster Press, 1961), 171-79.

101. Milton, *Tetrachordon*, in *Complete Prose Works* (New Haven, Conn.: Yale University Press, 1959), 2:597.

102. Wagner, 48-49.

103. Records cited by Foster Rhea Dulles, *America Learns to Play: A History of Popular Recreation, 1607-1940* (New York: Appleton Century, 1940), 6.

104. Ibid., 6.

105. Ibid.

106. Francis White, quoted in Wagner, 45.

107. William Burkitt, *The Poor Man's Help*, as quoted in Wagner, 50.

108. Baxter, *Christian Directory*, as quoted in Sasek, 114.

109. Baxter, *Christian Directory*, as quoted in Weber, 261.

PART 2

WORK AND LEISURE IN CHRISTIAN PERSPECTIVE

Chapter 5

A Christian Theology of Work

*T*he previous chapters have outlined an agenda of topics that are basic to any informed discussion of work and leisure. In the second half of the book we will integrate those topics with the Christian faith, bringing together the human data regarding work and leisure and Christian belief and experience.

Much depends, of course, on what we mean by "the Christian faith." Our view of the authority from which we derive our concept of Christianity at once places us in one or another Christian tradition. I write as an evangelical Christian for whom the Bible is the final authority for determining what is Christian. I have also drawn upon the insights of Christian thinkers and writers who have interpreted biblical principles in helpful ways.

One other explanation will clarify how I have proceeded. For both work and leisure, I have divided the material into a theological part and an ethical or moral part. The theology of work and leisure is concerned especially with broad Christian *doctrines* that provide a framework for understanding work and leisure. To speak of the ethics of work and leisure is to shift the focus to human *behavior* in these areas. Here we will

119

be primarily concerned with specific virtues and vices that people practice in regard to work and leisure.

In this chapter we will explore the broad theological foundation of a Christian view of work. The general outline is familiar to theology in general, consisting of creation, fall, and redemption. In this context, *redemption* refers to those Christian ideas that can redeem work from the curse it was subjected to after the Fall. We will also consider carefully the sacred-secular dichotomy, the concept of vocation or calling, and stewardship.

IN THE BEGINNING: WORK AND THE CREATED ORDER

Many writers on the subject of work trace the biblical data back to the curse that befell work after the Fall in Genesis 3. More enlightened writers trace it back to the work that God gave man in Paradise in Genesis 2. But the biblical view of work goes back even farther than this to the work of God as narrated in Genesis 1.

The Work of God

Work in the Bible begins with God's work of creation. God's work of creation is obviously not toil. It is more like play or the exuberance of the creative artist. It is joyous and energetic, unencumbered by the need to overcome obstacles or wrestle the physical elements into a finished product.

Yet the activity of God in creating the world must be considered work. We know, for example, that after six days of creation "God finished his work which he had done, and he rested on the seventh day from all his work which he had done" (Genesis 2:2). In the actual account of creation, moreover, God rests from his creative work after each day, setting up a rhythm of work and rest.

The work God does when creating the world is described in human terms. God becomes a cosmic gardener, for example, when he is said to have planted a garden in Eden (Genesis 2:8). He made the firmament and heavenly bodies and animals.

He formed man from the dust of the ground (Genesis 2:7) and made woman from the rib of man (Genesis 2:21-22). In the Bible's creation story, God is a craftsman. Psalm 19:1 says that "the firmament proclaims his handiwork." Psalm 8:3 pictures the heavens as the work of God's fingers.

According to the Bible, God's work did not stop with the creation of the world. It continues throughout history. God neither slumbers nor sleeps but is always busy protecting his people (Psalm 121). If early Genesis portrays God as a cosmic gardener tending the world of nature, Psalm 104 (verses 10-22) extends that picture to God's active provision for nature throughout history. In a psalm describing God's acts of rescue, the psalmist writes that God is known "for his wonderful works to the sons of men!" (Psalm 107:8, 15, 21, 31). The works of God as described in the Bible fall into the categories of creation, providence, judgment, and redemption.

In the New Testament, Christ, too, is a worker. He was a carpenter until the age of thirty. During his public ministry, he spoke repeatedly of his work. "We must work the works of him who sent me," Jesus said (John 9:4). His food was "to do the will of him who sent me, and to accomplish his work" (John 4:34). "My Father is working still, and I am working," Jesus told the Jews (John 5:17).

"The God of the Bible," Paul Minear aptly notes, "is preeminently a worker."[1] What is the significance of this? It at once lends sanction and dignity to the very idea of work. We can contrast the biblical view to the Greek view on this very point. We noted earlier the contempt with which classical thinkers regarded ordinary work. This negative attitude correlated with their view of the gods as being above work. According to Hesiod, "At the beginning the generations of men lived on the earth far removed from evils of difficult toil. . . . Men of the Golden Age used to live like gods . . . free from cares, from labour and from grief."[2] Not only is the good life for people conceived as an absence of work; the gods are similarly exempt from active work. As someone has noted, "A glance at a Concordance will show by the very frequency of mentions of work throughout the Old Testament that the Greek idea of the indignity of work has no place whatever there."[3]

The work of God, even though it is unique, remains a model for human work. It affirms that work is good and Godlike in principle. The work of God is creative, orderly, and constructive. It is universal. It benefits people and other creatures. It declares the very nature of God and bears his imprint or signature. Human work can do no better than emulate God's work.

There is an additional principle that emerges from God's work of creation. When God "saw everything that he had made . . . behold, it was very good" (Genesis 1:31). The creation that God made and declared good in principle is the God-given sphere in which people do their work. If "the earth is the LORD's and the fulness thereof, the world and those who dwell therein" (Psalm 24:1), then people's ordinary work in the world can be God's work. By removing any stigma from the material world itself, the Christian doctrine of creation also takes away the reproach that other traditions have placed upon earthly work. The Christian doctrine of creation at once renders impossible any dichotomy between the earthly and the sacred. The world has value to God and therefore to his creatures who live and work in it.

The Image of God in People

A second key idea that emerges from the Bible's creation account is that the God who works made people in his image (Genesis 1:26-27). No doubt many things make up this resemblance between God and his human creatures. But one obvious similarity between God and people made in his image is that they are both workers. This link between God's work and human work is made explicit in the fourth commandment of the Decalogue:

> Six days you shall labor, and do all your work. . . .
> For in six days the LORD made heaven and earth,
> the sea, and all that is in them (Exodus 20:9, 11).

People work because the God who created them in his image works. Human work has meaning partly because it expresses the divine image in people.

It follows that human work should share the nature of God's work. God worked not because he had to but because he wanted to. The song of the elders around God's throne stresses this: "thou didst create all things, and by thy will [KJV: for thy pleasure] they . . . were created" (Revelation 4:11). Dorothy Sayers wrote the following in a famous essay exploring the implications of the divine image in people:

> [Work] should . . . be thought of as a creative activity, undertaken for the love of the work itself; and . . . man, made in God's image, should make things, as God makes them, for the sake of doing well a thing that is well worth doing. . . . Work is the natural exercise and function of man—the creature who is made in the image of his Creator.[4]

Work as a Creation Ordinance

It is an easy step from the image of God in people to the idea that work is a creation ordinance. The usual term for it is *the creation mandate*. In creating man and woman in his image, God commanded, "Let them have dominion . . . over all the earth" (Genesis 1:26). To rule the earthly order of course involves work.

As interpreted by Christian theologians, the command to have dominion over the earth is more than an agricultural command. It does, of course, involve the control and nurture of the physical environment. But it is also a *cultural mandate*— a command by God to work through culture and civilization as well as to till the ground.

The very fact that God commanded such work shows that human work is part of the divine plan for history. It is a human necessity in the eyes of God. Alan Richardson notes in *The Biblical Doctrine of Work* that the teaching of the Old Testament on the subject of work may be generally summed up by saying that it is regarded as a necessary and indeed God-appointed function of human life. Since to labour is the common lot of mankind, it is important that men should accept it without complaining and thus fulfil with cheerful obedience the intention of the Creator for human existence. . . . The basic assumption of the biblical viewpoint is that work is a divine ordinance for the life of man. As such it falls within the sphere of . . . natural law.[5]

The link that the Bible draws between work and God's creation of the world confirms that work has the character of a natural law. Like gravity, it is simply one of the "givens" of the world God created. We can legitimately speak of work as a natural duty and right of the human race. It is a natural law for human existence and an expectation that God has laid on the human race as part of the created order.

Psalm 104 confirms this. It is a nature psalm that praises the provisions God has made for his natural creation. The section devoted to the sun and moon (vv. 19-23) focuses on the natural rhythm of day and night that orders the activities of people and animals. "When the sun rises," we read, "man goes forth to his work and to his labor until the evening." The point is clear: work is as much a part of the natural order as the rising of the sun. The corollary of this is that failure to work, whether through a person's choice or circumstances beyond one's control, is abnormal and unnatural.

To regard work as a creation mandate and a natural law invests it with dignity. To work is to carry on God's delegated task for creation, making the fullness of creation fuller. This also supplies the proper motivation for work:

This is the reason man should work today—not merely to make a living, not to gain luxuries, nor to "succeed" in the eyes of the world—but because it is God's plan for man to subjugate the earth. . . .

Such an interpretation of daily work enables us to realize that our contribution, however small it may appear, fits into God's pattern for developing the world. . . . All honorable work, no matter how insignificant before men, offers some opportunity to subdue this earth to God's will.[6]

Work in Paradise

In the classical tradition, work entered the world as a curse and punishment. It did not exist in the Golden Age. The biblical tradition is sometimes misrepresented as having the same attitude, but this is false. According to Genesis 2:15, work was part of God's perfect provision in Paradise: "The LORD God took the man and put him in the garden of Eden to till it and keep it."

The original Protestants made much of this verse, and rightly so. It shows clearly that work is part of God's original purpose for human life. Idleness is not the goal of human life, contrary to the Greek view of the state of innocence as endless leisure. In this we can see a pattern of what God intended for people. The Puritan John Robinson wrote, "God, who would have our first father, even in innocency . . . to labour . . . would have none of his posterity lead their life in idleness."[7]

John Milton's portrayal of life in Paradise (*Paradise Lost*, Book 4) is true to the spirit of biblical teaching and at the same time epitomizes the Puritan view of work. Milton repeatedly emphasizes that work in Paradise was not only pleasant but also necessary. Someone who made a thorough comparison of Milton's paradisal vision with those of earlier writers found that to portray work as necessary was "the most strikingly original feature of Milton's treatment."[8] There is no better summary of the biblically based Protestant work ethic than these words of Adam to Eve in Milton's poem:

Man hath his daily work of body or mind
Appointed, which declares his dignity,
And the regard of Heaven on all his ways.[9]

Here, in kernel form, is the original Puritan ethic: work is appointed by God, is the arena within which people live as stewards under God's oversight, and is part of the dignity that God conferred on the human race.

Divine and Human Work in Cooperation

One more thought must be added to the intertwined ideas of God's work, the image of God in people, and work as a creation ordinance that expresses God's original intention for people. It is the concept of God's work and human work as a cooperative partnership. We noted earlier that the work of God continues in nature and human history. Since God is sovereign, no human work can exist outside of his control. The modern notion of the self-made person is an impossibility. But people can become partners with God, carrying on his delegated work.

This attitude is encapsulated in Psalm 127:1:

> Unless the LORD builds the house,
>   those who build it labor in vain.

We should notice first that work itself is not disparaged here. What is declared futile is human labor apart from God's assistance. We note further that work itself is insufficient. What matters is the attitude of the worker toward God. That attitude, we infer, should be one of dependence, service, and worship. Within such a stance of humility, human work has dignity as a cooperative effort with God. God works through the worker, at once transforming human labor into something exalted, even spiritual.[10]

This blend of human and divine work appears at the end of Psalm 90 (vv. 16-17):

> Let thy work be manifest to thy servants,
>   and thy glorious power to their children.
> Let the favor of the Lord our God be upon us,
>   and establish thou the work of our hands upon us,
>   yea, the work of our hands establish thou it.

Again we find that the work of God is bigger than human work. As the writer of Ecclesiastes expresses it, "Consider the work of God; / who can make straight what he has made crooked?" (Ecclesiastes 7:13). But within this acknowledgment of God's sovereignty over the worker's life, people can legitimately pray that God will establish or bless the work of their hands. Human work is potentially small or great, depending on whether the worker invites God into his or her life as a sovereign partner.

If we want a pattern for this divine-human cooperation in work, consider the rebuilding of the wall of Jerusalem as recounted in the book of Nehemiah. The project rested partly on human initiative: "all the wall was joined together to half its height. For the people had a mind to work" (Nehemiah 4:6). When Nehemiah's enemies tried to divert him from his work, his response showed the importance he attached to the physical work of building a wall: "I am doing a great work and I cannot come down. Why should the work stop while I leave it and come down to you?" (6:3).

But Nehemiah's work was more than a human effort. When enemies tried to frighten the workers, saying to themselves that "their hands will drop from the work," Nehemiah prayed, "But now, O God, strengthen thou my hands" (Nehemiah 6:9). When the work was finished, moreover, Nehemiah offered an assessment that balanced his earlier commendation of the people because they "had a mind to work." The enemies were afraid, Nehemiah wrote, "for they perceived that this work had been accomplished with the help of our God" (6:16). Much the same can be said of all honorable work, whether or not the worker acknowledges the help of God.

Luther's concept of vocation made much of this human-divine cooperation in work.[11] According to Luther, when we carry out our vocation in faith to God and obedience to his commands, God will work through us. Such a view of work saves us both from the paralyzing fear of human ineffectiveness and from arrogance over human achievement. We have no

ability of our own, independent of God. But when we accept
the power of God in our lives, our work becomes God's work.
In the words of Luther, God's blessings

> at times come to us through our labors and at times
> without our labors, but never because of our labors;
> for God always gives them because of His unde-
> served mercy. . . . He uses our labor as a sort of
> mask, under the cover of which he blesses us and
> grants us what is His, so that there is room for faith.[12]

In our day, John Stott has written,

> This concept of divine-human collaboration applies
> to all honorable work. God has so ordered life on
> earth as to depend on us. . . . So whatever our
> work, we need to see it as being . . . cooperation
> with God. . . . It is this that glorifies him.[13]

Summary

A biblical understanding of work reaches back to the very
beginning of the world. As we look at the doctrine of creation,
we find human work placed into a context of God's work, of
human creation in the image of God, of God's command for
people to work as part of his provision for human life, and of
human cooperation with God in work.

BY THE SWEAT OF YOUR BROW: WORK AS A CURSE

The second chapter in the biblical history of work, often
mistakenly said to be the first chapter, is much simpler than
the opening. It is rooted in the Christian doctrine of the fall
of the human race from innocence to sin.

Work and the Fall

We have seen that work was an important part of God's
perfect provision for Adam and Eve in their state of innocence.
It gave purpose to their lives. Work also figures prominently

in the story of human life after the Fall. Whereas work before the Fall was a blessing, after the Fall it became a curse (Genesis 3:17-19):

> cursed is the ground because of you;
> in toil you shall eat of it all the days of your life;
> thorns and thistles it shall bring forth to you;
> and you shall eat the plants of the field.
> In the sweat of your face
> you shall eat bread
> till you return to the ground.

We should note several things about this key passage. First, the Fall changed work but did not cancel work as a duty imposed by God on the human race. God still commanded Adam and his posterity to work.

Second, the Fall did not introduce work into the world. Work as a blessing was already present. The new element is that work has now become a curse. It is, more specifically, a punishment that people bear as a burden. Something that was originally good has been perverted from its original perfection.

The new element is that work has become toil—something that must be accomplished against the hostility of the environment in which work occurs. Work originally served a purpose of human fulfillment, but it is now a source of frustration. Forrester comments that "man was meant to be a gardener, but by reason of his sin he became a farmer."[14] Work in a fallen world has the character of striving against forces that resist the worker's efforts. As twentieth-century British poet William Butler Yeats puts it in his poem *Adam's Curse*, "It's certain there is no fine thing / Since Adam's fall but needs much labouring."

In the story of the Fall, woman's pain in childbearing (Genesis 3:16) is a parallel curse to the toil of work (v. 17). Forrester comments that the Hebrew word for toil and pain in these verses is the same, adding, "It is worth noting how in language after language the same word is used for toil and child-bearing, e.g., 'labour' and 'travail.'"[15]

After the Fall

The biblical book that speaks most powerfully about the curse that work can be in a fallen world is the book of Ecclesiastes. It contains haunting pictures of the emptiness and futility of work "under the sun," that is, work pursued apart from the God-centered life. In these negative sections of Ecclesiastes, we get a virtual anatomy of what goes wrong with work. When the speaker attempts to find satisfaction in acquiring more and more goods (Ecclesiastes 2:1-10), he reaches a dead end: "Then I considered all that my hands had done and the toil I had spent in doing it, and behold, all was vanity and a striving after wind" (Ecclesiastes 2:11). Here, in poetic eloquence, is the rat race of work.

The Preacher also undertook a quest to find meaning in work itself, only to admit failure in the end:

> I hated all my toil in which I had toiled under the sun. . . . What has a man from all the toil and strain with which he toils beneath the sun? For all his days are full of pain, and his work is a vexation; even in the night his mind does not rest (Ecclesiastes 2:18, 22-23).

The book of Ecclesiastes here expresses in universal terms what we individually experience in our own lives. For variations on the theme, we can turn to the contemporary data cited in an earlier chapter. In fact, the interviews that Studs Terkel conducted for his book *Working* tell us in detail what the writer of Ecclesiastes says with the conciseness of proverbs. The Christian doctrine of the Fall explains what lies behind the phenomenon of unfulfilling and difficult work. The curse pronounced by God to Adam still echoes in human ears.

I was once asked by a troubled student whether work should not always be inherently fulfilling for a Christian. Should we feel guilty when work is burdensome to us? The effect of the Fall on work is that work is not always inherently rewarding.

In fact, God pronounced a curse on it. Many of the tasks we perform in a fallen world are inherently distasteful and wearisome. At this point the original Protestant ethic lets us down. Those who preached and wrote on the subject of work overrated it, acting as though it were not a curse at all.

The Abuses of Work

Not only did work become drudgery as a result of the Fall; it also became subject to abuse. The evidence comes from two sources. We can simply listen to the news and look around us to see that work has become perverted. The Bible likewise paints an ever-expanding picture of the vices that became associated with work after the Fall, as we will see in the next chapter.

The abuses take many forms. One is idleness, the refusal to accept the duty of work. Another is overwork, destructive to both the worker and his family. Labor is often forced upon people to their detriment and to the dishonest gain of those who exploit the worker. Some work is dishonest or immoral, and much of it is directed to produce goods and services that are useless or ignoble.

Summary

Work neither began nor ceased with the fall of the human race. It simply took a different shape. It became a curse rather than an unmitigated blessing. This is simply a "given" of life as we know it. At this point the Bible shows a thoroughgoing realism about work.

But the whole pattern of Christian theology is to offer a solution to the problems occasioned by sin. Work can be redeemed, even in a fallen world. Anything that helps us to overcome the effects of sin on work is part of this redemption. Work itself retains some of the quality of a curse, but the attitude of the worker can transform it.

THE EARTH IS THE LORD'S:
REJECTING THE SACRED-SECULAR DICHOTOMY

The reclamation of work in a fallen world begins where the Protestant ethic began—by declaring the sanctity of all legitimate work in the world, no matter how common. This means that no vocation, including church work, is regarded as more "spiritual" or more pleasing to God than ordinary types of work. We must remember too that work is much broader than simply one's job. If work in this broader sense is to be redeemed in our thinking and doing, we obviously need a view of the goodness of mundane work.

There is abundant biblical support for the Reformation's view that all of life is God's and that common life in the world can be glorifying to God. The principle itself is stated as a command: "So, whether you eat or drink, or whatever you do, do all to the glory of God" (1 Corinthians 10:31). Eating and drinking are thoroughly physical and earthly activities, yet they can glorify God.

This obviously opens the door for all types of work to be glorifying to God as well. This is how the Bible portrays work. Paul wrote to Titus to remind Christians "to be ready for any honest work" (Titus 3:1).

Paul himself practiced what he preached. He was called to be an apostle, yet even in that calling he remained a tentmaker as a way of earning his livelihood. One could not ask for a better illustration of the Protestant rejection of the sacred-secular dichotomy. Paul could have become a professional cleric but refused to do so (see 1 Corinthians 9:3-18; 2 Thessalonians 3:7-9). Furthermore, as Richardson notes, "It is assumed throughout the New Testament that daily work, so far from being a hindrance to Christian living, is a necessary ingredient of it."[16]

Common Work in the Bible

The dignity of common work is established in the Bible not so much by specific proof texts as by the general picture of life that emerges. As we read the Bible we find a veritable gallery of people engaged in the ordinary work of life. Many biblical characters are known to us by their occupations. There are soldiers, chariot drivers, garment makers, farmers, merchants, and judges.

We see King Saul not only as a king but also a farmer plowing with his oxen in the field (1 Samuel 11:5). His successor David was a shepherd:

> [God] chose David his servant,
> and took him from the sheepfolds;
> from tending the ewes that had young he brought him
> to be the shepherd of Jacob his people,
> of Israel his inheritance.
> With upright heart he tended them,
> and guided them with skilful hand (Psalm 78:70-72).

Here we find no hierarchy of occupations in the sight of God. Tending sheep or a nation has the same validity.

The list of God-ordained occupations keeps expanding as we read the Bible. God called Abraham to be a wandering pilgrim, which at the same time entailed being a nomadic shepherd. God called Bezalel to be an artist (Exodus 31:1-5), Moses to be a national leader. We find lists of people who mixed the spices and made the flat cakes for worship in the temple (1 Chronicles 9). Ruth was a farmer's wife and mother, greatly blessed by God in her common work. Richardson summarizes the picture thus:

> The Hebrews looked upon daily work as a normal part of the divine ordering of the world, and no man was exempt from it. . . . No stigma is attached to being a "worker" in the Old Testament; on the contrary, it is expected that every man will have his proper work to do.[17]

This assessment is confirmed by Paul Minear's analysis

of Psalm 127:1, which talks about the work of the housebuilder and the watchman:

> The Psalmist . . . does not draw up a list of preferred occupations which God approves. . . . He does not discuss the merits of masonry as over against those of army life. He focuses attention upon the persons who work. . . . The teaching [that the Psalmist states in this verse] is relevant to all types of work, and to every worker in his own employment. . . . His work is endowed with a significance that goes far beyond the visible results of that work. . . . By placing the accent on the person who labors, the Psalmist gives to every kind of work a genuine . . . significance.[18]

The Example of Jesus

The same regard for the sanctity of the common can be seen in the life of Jesus. His vocation during most of his life was that of a carpenter. The early Puritan Hugh Latimer commented,

> Our Saviour Christ before he began his preaching . . . was a carpenter, and got his living with great labor. Therefore let no man disdain . . . to follow him in a . . . common calling and occupation. For as he blessed our nature with taking upon him the shape of man, so in his doing he blessed all occupations and arts.[19]

The same feeling for common occupations emerges from the discourses and parables of Jesus. Jesus repeatedly showed his familiarity with the common world of breadbaking, sowing, harvesting, fishing, tending sheep, and caring for a vineyard. Here, as elsewhere in the Bible, we find no cleavage of life into sacred and secular. It is assumed rather that the commonplace is sacred.

Protestant Glorification of Earthly Work

In view of the biblical data, it is clear that the Reformers and Puritans were right in their rejection of the two-world mentality that made work in the world second-best. Whereas the Catholic tradition had tended to make acts of spiritual contemplation and devotion the sphere in which a person can find God, the goal of the Reformation was to bring the spiritual world into everyday life. It is in the shop, wrote the Puritan Richard Steele, "where you may most confidently expect the presence and blessing of God."[20]

The two-world mentality has a tendency to make life in the world exempt from Christian spirituality. But the Protestant tradition, in keeping with what we find in the Bible, exempts no part of life from Christian standards. The American Puritan John Cotton claimed, "Not only my spiritual life but even my civil life in this world, all the life I live, is by the faith of the Son of God: He exempts no life from the agency of His faith."[21]

A final conclusion that follows from this rejection of the two-world model is that the earthly arena takes on a sense of ultimacy. As in Jesus' parables and the Bible generally, early Protestantism made it clear that the spiritual issues of life are determined in the here and now, not in some other spiritual world. A scholar of Luther has noted that Luther often used the imagery of "below" or "down here" when talking about vocation.[22] Christian service to God does not occur in a "sacred" place such as a church, but in the everyday routine. As Luther put it, if we viewed the matter aright, "the entire world would be full of service to God, not only the churches but also the home, the kitchen, the cellar, the workshop, and the field of the townsfolk and farmers."[23]

The Practical Result

This doctrine of the sanctity of common labor has immense implications for our daily living, beginning with our jobs. Anxiety among Christians about their job does not reach only to people with menial jobs, though it certainly includes them. I have known wealthy, successful Christians with financially prestigious jobs who felt guilty because their work seemed far removed from "Kingdom service." There are, of course, jobs about which one should feel guilty. But any job that serves humanity and in which one can glorify God is a Kingdom job.

The Christian glorification of common labor also obliterates the social distinctions that society at large puts on occupations. In general, occupations that pay well or involve power are high on the ladder of prestige. Menial or poor paying jobs are stigmatized. This hierarchy of value with regard to work has an insidious way of infiltrating churches and boards of Christian organizations. I have heard of churches where the session consists wholly of successful professional people and where their professional accomplishments are flaunted at the time of their election to office.

The biblical view of the worthiness of all legitimate occupations shows that such an attitude is wrong. In God's sight, a banker or businessman is not engaged in more important work than a carpenter or housewife.

Finally, the Christian attitude toward common work comes as good news regarding the work we do off the job. Here, in fact, is where we tend to have particularly bad attitudes toward work because it is unpaid work. God is interested in our washing the clothes and painting the house. In the words of Luther, "What you do in your house is worth as much as if you did it up in heaven for our Lord God."[24]

WORK AS A CALLING

A second major pillar in the reclamation of work from the curse is the Christian doctrine of vocation or calling. It is an immense subject on which (again) the early Protestants will be our best guide. The Reformers and Puritans spoke of two callings, and this is our necessary starting point.

The Call to Salvation, Godliness, and Discipleship

God first of all calls people to a godly life. This general calling takes precedence over everything else, including our work. The Bible speaks frequently of the call to the godly life. For example, God called Abraham to leave a settled life and follow his leading "to the land that I will show you" (Genesis 12:1). In his book *Christian Vocation*, W. R. Forrester argues that "Abraham was the first man with a definite, explicit sense of vocation. 'Faith' ever afterwards was a response to a 'call' from God."[25]

The call to Abraham subsequently became a general call to the Old Testament nation of Israel to follow God, and again it was primarily a spiritual call. It was, moreover, a corporate call:

> This establishment of God's covenant with Israel made the corporate vocation the primary basis for each person's vocation. Wherever an individual was given a specific mission, he was in one way or another carrying forward the mission of the whole community. Wherever the community was assigned a task, implicit in it was a vocation for every person within the community.[26]

The call to accept God's salvation and follow him in a life of spiritual service permeates the New Testament as well. It no longer applies to an entire nation but to the individuals who make up the body of Christ.

Examples abound. Paul wrote to Timothy about "the eternal life to which you were called when you made the good confession" (1 Timothy 6:12). He wrote to the Corinthians about being "called into the fellowship of [God's] Son, Jesus Christ our Lord" (1 Corinthians 1:9), and to the Thessalonians about being "called . . . through our gospel" to "be saved, through sanctification by the Spirit and belief in the truth" (2 Thessalonians 2:13, 14). Christians are "called . . . out of darkness into [God's] marvelous light" (1 Peter 2:9). They are also "called in the one body" of believers (Colossians 3:15) and are "called to be saints" (1 Corinthians 1:2).

The call to be followers of God in the spiritual life of salvation and sanctification may seem a long way from the subject of work, but it is not. It reminds us of the primacy of the spiritual in all of life. It puts work in its place. Work is not the most important thing in life. Being a Christian is.

The Puritans were very clear on this point. They elevated the general call to the Christian life over the specific call to tasks and occupations. William Perkins wrote, for example, that "the particular calling of any man is inferior to the general calling of a Christian: and when they cannot both stand together, the particular calling must give place; because we are bound unto God in the first place."[27]

The Call to Religious Service

A second category of calling that the Bible describes is the calling to specific spiritual tasks or offices. As I say that, I am already aware of a certain ambiguity about what constitutes "spiritual" tasks. I will use the term to mean such tasks as prophesying in God's name, preaching the gospel, or filling an office in the church.

The Old Testament prophets and priests were called by God to proclaim messages from God. Isaiah, for example, received a vision of God and heard "the voice of him who called" (Isaiah 6:1-10). God "took" Amos "from following the flock, and . . . said . . . 'Go, prophesy to my people Israel'" (Amos 7:15). God also set apart the Levites to perform the priestly duties of Old Testament worship (Numbers 18:1-7).

A similar pattern exists in the New Testament, although the offices themselves have changed. The Gospels record how Jesus called his disciples to the office of apostle. In a similar way, Paul begins most of his epistles by asserting that he has been called to be an apostle. Here is a typical example: "Paul, called by the will of God to be an apostle of Christ Jesus" (1 Corinthians 1:1). Elsewhere Paul claims that he was "appointed a preacher and apostle and teacher" (2 Timothy 1:11). Within these offices, he was called to the specific task of preaching, as we discover from his statement in Acts 16:10 that "God had called us to preach the gospel."

In the New Testament we also read about specific church offices to which God calls people. In Ephesians 4:11 we read that God's "gifts were that some should be apostles, some prophets, some evangelists, some pastors and teachers." A parallel passage mentions apostles, prophets, teachers, workers of miracles, healers, helpers, administrators, and speakers in tongues (1 Corinthians 12:28).

From such references we can conclude that God calls some people to specific spiritual ministries within the church. These ministries can be either offices (careers) or tasks. Applied to the subject of work, this means that in God's design some people are called to tasks and occupations that are specifically religious or church-related. This still leaves most occupations and tasks unaccounted for.

Are Ordinary Work and Occupations Also a Calling?

The important question thus becomes, What about ordinary work and occupations? Can they also be regarded as a calling from God?

This question has been a point of immense disagreement through the centuries. A study of the history of the word *vocation* reveals that in the early Christian centuries, only those who renounced ordinary occupations and entered "the church" (broadly defined to include monasteries) were considered to have a calling from God.[28] Only with the advance of the Reformation was the concept of vocation extended beyond church offices and specific acts to general occupations and their related activities in the world. The history of the word "thus shows a complete reversal of its meaning. At first it meant, the monk alone has a calling; Luther says just the reverse, it is exactly monasticism which has no calling; the genuine calling of God realizes itself within the world and its work."[29]

Was the Reformation right in its claim? I believe the Bible supports the idea that ordinary occupations and tasks are something to which God calls people, even though the phraseology is not always specifically that of calling.

For example, God called Moses to lead the nation of Israel (Exodus 3-4). What kind of office was this? It was certainly more than a religious office. It was also what we would call a political office of national leadership. God similarly "chose" David and "took him from the sheepfolds" to be the king of Israel (Psalm 78:70-71). When Samuel confronted King Saul at Gilgal, he reminded him that "the Lord anointed you king over Israel" (1 Samuel 15:17). In the Old Testament, national leadership was a calling from God.

The same sense of calling by God extends to the artists who did the art work for the tabernacle. The terminology could not be more clear:

> The LORD said to Moses, "See, I have called by name Bezalel . . . and I have filled him with the Spirit of God, with ability and intelligence, with knowledge and all craftsmanship, to devise artistic designs, to work in gold, silver, and bronze, in cutting stones for setting, and in carving wood, for work in every craft. And behold, I have appointed with him Oholiab . . . and I have given to all able men ability, that they may make all that I have commanded you" (Exodus 31:1-6).

When Moses recounts this message to the Israelites, he likewise treats the artists' work as a calling:

> "See, the LORD has called by name Bezalel . . . and he has filled him with the Spirit of God, with ability, with intelligence, with knowledge, and with all craftsmanship, to devise artistic designs, to work in gold and silver and bronze, in cutting stones for setting, and in carving wood, for work in every skilled craft. And he has inspired him to teach, both

> him and Oholiab. . . . He has filled them with ability to do every sort of work done by a craftsman or by a designer or by an embroiderer . . . or by a weaver—by any sort of workman or skilled designer" (Exodus 35:30-35).

Here the concept of calling is clearly applied to a range of occupations, including art and teaching.

There is also a more general line of evidence in the Bible. It is simply that God's providence led his people to have occupations in the world. God called Abraham to follow him, but this did not mean that Abraham ceased to give his daily attention to the work of tending his flocks and herds. The Twelve followed Jesus but also continued to fish. Although Paul was called to be an apostle, he continued to be a tentmaker as a way of earning his living (1 Corinthians 9:12-15). He did not speak of tentmaking as a calling, but there is no evidence that he regarded it as any less pleasing to God than his preaching.

An office or task does not have to be termed a calling in order to be regarded as such. The picture that emerges from the Bible is that God arranged society in such a way that there are farmers, housewives, hunters, soldiers, kings, chariot drivers, and dye makers. His providence, moreover, leads people into one or another of these. If they are not callings from God, what are they? If they are unworthy of people, why did God arrange things in such a way that people have to do them?

The key biblical text in this regard has unfortunately produced competing interpretations. It is found in 1 Corinthians 7:

> Let every one lead the life which the Lord has assigned to him, and in which God has called him. . . . Every one should remain in the state [KJV, "calling"] in which he was called (vv. 17, 20).

Some interpreters believe that the calling in which Christians are to remain is the Christian life, and that it has nothing to do with occupation. I disagree. The context makes it clear that Paul is raising the issue of how conversion should affect one's everyday life. His answer: it does not affect one's external role or station in life at all. Christians should remain married (1 Corinthians 7:10-16), should remain circumcised or uncircumcised (vv. 18-19), should remain slaves until given the opportunity to gain their freedom (vv. 21-24).

By *calling* Paul obviously means our external situation, not the inner spiritual life. Paul has no reason to command new Christians to remain a Christian. That is not even open to question. The surrounding context makes it clear that the question to which he speaks is whether new Christians should abandon their family situation or occupation.

Fortunately we have a parallel passage in the gospels. When converts asked John the Baptist what they should do in regard to their occupation, he implied that they should remain in it, provided they could be honest in such a vocation:

> Tax collectors also came to be baptized, and said to him, "Teacher, what shall we do?" And he said to them, "Collect no more than is appointed you." Soldiers also asked him, "And we, what shall we do?" And he said to them, "Rob no one by violence or by false accusation, and be content with your wages" (Luke 3:12-14).

The point is clear: the Christian life infuses moral and spiritual values into earthly occupations, but the occupations themselves retain their integrity.

Paul's command to remain in the calling to which one has been called is a key to understanding the biblical teaching about ordinary occupations. The Reformers were right in stressing it. It was a revolutionary idea for the Greek world. One scholar claims that Paul is forced to use the word *calling* in an entirely new sense from its customary use in order to express the idea that one's work in the world is just as much a calling from God as the call to the Christian life.[30]

Wade Boggs agrees with this interpretation and cites others who are of the same mind.[31] As Boggs notes, when Paul speaks

of the new convert's remaining in "the calling wherein he was
called" (KJV), he

> uses the same Greek stem in two different senses.
> The second is the usual New Testament meaning
> and refers to the summons by which Christians are
> "called" into God's Kingdom. The first is defined
> by the context as meaning one's station or status in
> life as married or unmarried (vv. 25-29), circumcised
> or uncircumcised (vv. 18-19), bond or free (vv. 21-
> 23), buyer or seller (vv. 30-31).

Furthermore, notes Boggs, this understanding of ordinary work
and occupations as a calling from God accords with such broad
biblical doctrines as the sovereignty of God over all of a person's
life, the providence of God that directs a person's life, the
Lordship of Christ over every aspect of a Christian's life, work
as something delegated to the human race by God at the time
of creation, and a person's stewardship of what God has given
him.

Christian Calling: A Necessary Foundation

Unless we place work into the context of Christian calling,
we have little to say about a Christian view of occupations.
If, however, we agree that work in general and occupations in
particular can be viewed in terms of Christian calling, we can
proceed to explore what this means in practical terms.

As I conduct that exploration, I want to make it clear that
work involves much more than one's job. It encompasses the
whole range of tasks and duties that attach themselves to the
roles God has given us, all the way from putting in our time
on the job to driving children to music lessons. In the words
of Calvin, God "has assigned distinct duties to each in the
different modes of life."[32] Perkins spoke in similar terms when
he described a calling as "a certain manner of leading our lives
in this world."[33]

God Is the One Who Calls

The doctrine of calling implies that someone does the calling. "Someone" is of course God. Calvin said simply that a person's calling "is connected with God, who actually calls us."[34] Perkins elaborated the concept:

> God is the general, appointing to every man his particular calling and as it were his standing. . . . God himself is the author and beginning of callings. This overthroweth the heathenish opinion of men, which think that the particular condition and state of man in this life comes by chance, or by the bare will and pleasure of man himself.[35]

If God is the one who calls people to their tasks, it follows that God wants people to work. As we have already seen, work is a creation ordinance, a command from God. This has important consequences. Can a person who is underemployed or trapped in unfulfilling work regard such work as a calling? The answer is yes. If God wants people to work—if this is the minimal condition for a calling—then work as opposed to idleness is a calling. Of course we have reason to wish for more than the minimum.

Work as a Response to God

To view work as a calling at once makes it something personal. If God calls us to work, then to do the work is to obey God. That is why the Reformers made so much of the attitude of the worker. Work becomes a calling only if we recognize God's hand in it and view it as part of our relationship with God. Here is a specimen statement by Luther:

> If you ask an insignificant maidservant why she scours a dish or milks the cow she can say: I know that the thing I do pleases God, *for I have God's word and commandment.* . . . God does not look at the insignificance of the acts *but at the heart that serves Him* in such little things [italics mine].[36]

As the italicized phrases show, it makes all the difference in the world when we regard work as a call from God. Viewing it that way provides a spiritual context of faith and obedience within which to do our work.

Work thus ideally becomes service, a means of glorifying God. The American Puritan John Cotton described it thus:

> We live by faith in our vocations. . . . A man therefore . . . doth his work sincerely as in God's presence, and as one that hath a heavenly business in hand, and therefore comfortably knowing God approves of his way and work.[37]

The Significance of All Legitimate Work

Another corollary that follows from the idea of work as a calling is that it puts all work on the same plane of spiritual significance. The doctrine of vocation is a great equalizer, and there is something radically democratic about it.

In analyzing the biblical concept of vocation, Minear notes,

> One effect of this was to give workers in all trades a genuine equality before God and a genuine importance in the life of the community. . . . Equality was thus posited not on the basis of an immediate appeal to inherited rights or social utility but by reference to the horizons of God's call. . . . No menial work was in itself beneath the dignity of prophet, priest, or king. In fact, God chose an obscure shepherd boy as king and an unheralded carpenter as Messiah.[38]

If every task or job is a calling from God, its value is independent of the prestige games the human race is always busy playing. The Christian concept of calling liberates us from bondage to human value systems and is a rebuke to people who use those systems to feed their pride.

Contentment with One's Work

Yet another practical result of viewing work as a calling from God is the potential it carries for inducing contentment and patience in work. This too is part of the redemption that Christian vocation brings to the curse and drudgery of work. Tasks such as preparing surfaces for painting or typing letters all day or washing dishes do not carry their own reward. But if God calls us to such work, we suddenly have a reason to accept them with a degree of contentment.

The original Protestants made much of this. Cotton's statement may be taken as typical:

> Faith . . . encourageth a man in his calling to the most homely and difficult . . . things. . . . If faith apprehend this or that to be the way of my calling, it encourages me to it, though it be never so homely and difficult. . . . Such homely employments a carnal heart knows not how to submit unto; but now faith having put us into a calling, if it require some homely employment, it encourageth us to it.[39]

Cotton Mather wrote, "Is your business here clogged with any difficulties and inconveniences? Contentment under those difficulties is no little part of your homage to that God who hath placed you where you are."[40]

Loyalty to a Vocation

The original Protestants saw something else in the idea of calling that may not sit well with a society that conceives of work mainly in economic terms and that lives with images of upward mobility based on job changes in its mind. I happen to think the Reformers and Puritans were right. At the very least we should hear them out.

Calvin, for example, wrote this about 1 Corinthians 7:20:

> Each should be content with his calling and persist in it, and not be eager to change to something else. . . . [Paul] wishes to correct the thoughtless

> eagerness which impels some to change their situation without any proper reason. . . . He condemns the restlessness which prevents individuals from remaining contentedly as they are.[41]

Luther spoke slightingly of "fickle, unstable spirits" who "gape after that which has been committed and given to someone else" and therefore "cannot continue in their calling."[42] And Mather, while not questioning that a person could change occupation, nevertheless observed that "many a man, merely from covetousness and from discontent throws up his business."[43]

What is at stake here? Certainly much more than an overly conservative social theory. That part of it we can discard as excess baggage. But if we are going to take the idea of a calling from God seriously, modern notions of job become deficient.

The doctrine of vocation removes the element of arbitrariness from one's choice of work. For one thing, God's providence is seen as the force that arranged circumstances in such a way that a person has a particular work. God also equips a person with the necessary talents and abilities to perform the work. In fact, the original Protestants made this one of the tests to know whether one was in the right calling. God ordinarily blesses a person's calling with signs of approval and achievement.

Given this framework of God's sovereign activity in one's calling, how can people lightly turn their back on their vocation? If God has called us, how can we be anything other than faithful to that calling? A calling should be something with great dignity and stature in our thinking. It is not a mere job.

We also have to ask why people change their vocation with such ease in our day. They do so overwhelmingly for personal reasons. Usually they want a bigger paycheck. They follow the perennial impulse to think that the grass is greener somewhere else. Sometimes they are restless and lack purpose. Such reasons become suspect when placed into the framework of Christian vocation.

Calvin stated one other aspect to loyalty in one's calling

that I have found personally very useful. He compared a calling to a watchman or sentry that keeps a person from being distracted from his or her main business in life.[44] Thus conceived, a sense of calling can keep us on the path of our greatest service to God and society. Above all, it can allow us to say "no" to opportunities with a clear conscience.

Much of the overwork and sloppy work we sometimes find in Christian circles could be curbed if people stuck to their main calling or the task for which they are best suited and did not feel pressured to say yes to every request for their services. Dorothy Sayers put it this way: "When you find a man who is a Christian praising God by the excellence of his work—do not distract him and take him away from his proper vocation to address religious meetings and open church bazaars. Let him serve God in the way to which God has called him."[45]

The Practical Effect of Viewing Work as a Calling

The Christian doctrine of vocation comes as good news to all who work, especially those who do not have a church-related occupation. It opens the way to regard work not simply as the arena *within which* one serves God but *through which* one serves him.

There is a crucial difference between these two conceptions. Most Christians believe they can be a Christian at work. To do so involves being a diligent worker, being honest in one's dealings with an employer, and witnessing to fellow workers. But this still leaves the work itself untouched by one's Christian faith. The original Protestants were right in going beyond this and claiming that the work itself is a spiritual issue and a means of glorifying God. We can be Christian not only in our work but through our work if we view our work as an obedient response to God's calling.

How Do We Discover Our Vocation?

The Bible offers no explicit teaching on the question of how we can discover our vocation. The suggestions I am about to offer are my own thinking on the subject, as influenced by the research I did for this book and the views of the Reformers and Puritans.

At the most rudimentary level, our calling is the job that currently provides our livelihood, even if that job is temporary. As we will see in the next chapter, the Bible makes it plain that God expects people to provide for their needs through diligent work. God is honored by excellence in work. The job by which God is currently providing for our needs is our calling and as such worthy of our best effort. This is the minimal requirement a job or task must meet to rank as a proper vocation, assuming the job is itself morally legitimate.

But of course when we raise the question of how we know what our calling is, we usually presuppose that we can choose our vocation. When such is the case, our choice should be guided by the principles of effective service to God and society, maximum use of one's abilities and talents, and the providence or guidance of God as it is worked out through the circumstances of life. In none of these instances should we unduly mysticize the process by which God calls us. To discover our calling requires our best reason, research, and analysis.

To the extent we are free to choose our vocation, we should choose on the basis of the opportunities the job provides for service to God and people. No doubt we can have a Christian witness and meet people's needs in a wide range of vocations, but some jobs provide more opportunity for such service than others do. Christians should make career choices as citizens of God's kingdom first of all.

We also know that God has made us unique persons with our individual talents, interests, and temperament. God is glorified, and his purpose for our lives is fulfilled, when we pursue a vocation that meets our aptitudes. Within such a context of Christian stewardship (using the abilities God has given us), I believe the conventional criterion of self-fulfillment in our vocation is a legitimate test of whether we are in the right place. By the same criterion, lack of self-fulfillment or well-being is a good reason to reconsider our current occupation. Such an assessment must of course take into account the other criteria by which we choose a vocation (such as the ideal of serviceableness to God and society).

Discovering the vocation for which we are best suited may require aptitude tests and career counseling. These are God's appointed means of guiding us into the right vocation. They are made all the more necessary by the myriad occupations in our complex society. The advice of trustworthy acquaintances is likewise an indispensable source of counsel about where our talents lie.

In addition to the criteria of serviceableness and aptitude, we choose our vocation by following God's providence and arrangement of circumstances in our lives. It is obvious that many of the "choices" that lead to our vocation are made for us by God, through the agency of people and circumstances. The journey by which we arrive at any job is a series of opened and closed doors. Here we need to pray for God to lead us into the vocation and specific job of his choosing.

Once we're in a vocation or job, how do we know whether we should stay in it? By the same criteria I have urged for choosing a career. If we are of service to God and people, if our talents are being used, if we are fulfilled in our work, and if God through circumstances blesses our work with positive results, then we have every reason to believe we are in the right vocation. Conversely, if these things are lacking, we should question whether we are in the right place.

In proposing these criteria for discovering a vocation, I have avoided mysticizing the process. Personally I am skeptical when I hear people say with an aura of piety that they came to their current occupation because they "felt called by God," with the implication that it was not a reasoned or deliberate choice. Upon further questioning it turns out that either these people took the position without careful planning, or they followed the very human process of reasoning I have outlined. As with the other major decisions in our lives, God does not relieve us of the burden of human responsibility and choices. When asked how we came to our current occupation, I think we should have an explanation of exactly *how* God called us to that position, not simply a pious statement *that* he called us.

When we consider the question of our occupation, we must not lose sight of the big picture. As the Puritans insisted, our primary calling is to live a godly life. Our occupation is not the most important thing in life, though our own culture would have us believe that it is. No job that hinders our spiritual development can be the right one. And if the personal satisfaction we find in our job leaves a lot to be desired, we must remember that it is, after all, a secondary consideration to the life of faith and holiness.

In discussing vocation I have limited my remarks to the topic of occupation or career, but the early Protestants rightly conceived of our callings as being much broader than our job. All of our roles in life are callings. Being a spouse, a parent, a church member, a neighbor, and a Christian are all callings. These callings, too, are part of the big picture into which we must place our occupation. We should not make career choices without considering their impact on our other callings.

I have said nothing thus far about the level of pay as a criterion by which to choose an occupation. Economic considerations have been given an unduly high place by our secular society. According to surveys in recent years, the prospect of high salaries is a leading factor in the choices today's college students make regarding academic majors and careers. Salary considerations often take precedence over a student's aptitude and interests.

I see no justification for Christians to elevate salary over the considerations of service to God and society and maximum use of their God-given talents. I am not opposed to Christians making lots of money. If used properly, money can be a great blessing, while constant financial anxiety is usually detrimental to family happiness and even one's spiritual life. But I continue to believe that it is better to choose a vocation on the criteria

of serviceableness and aptitude than on the basis of a big
income.

WORK AS STEWARDSHIP

The Christian doctrines that all of life is God's and that
God calls people to their work are two mighty assaults against
the curse of work. A third Christian doctrine follows naturally
from the previous two. It is that the worker is a steward who
serves God.

A steward is a person who is entrusted with a master's
property. Applied to work, it means that the work we perform
in the world is given to us by God. To accomplish our work
is to serve God.

The Parable of the Stewards

The key biblical text is Jesus' parable of the talents
(Matthew 25:14-30). The story revolves around a master who
entrusted his talents (weights of money) to three stewards before
going on a long journey. Two of the stewards invested the
money wisely and doubled its amount during their master's
absence. The third servant, called "the wicked and slothful
servant," hid his entrusted money in the ground. Upon the
master's return, the industrious servants were rewarded, while
the slothful servant was cast into outer darkness.

This is obviously a metaphor or allegorical story about
stewardship in general. What it says about work cannot be
overemphasized. At least five principles emerge.[46]

To begin, the parable underscores the doctrine of vocation.
God is the sovereign provider of all opportunities, abilities,
and time for work. He provides the very materials for work.
Having provided the things that make work possible, he calls
people to work for him. The implication is clear: everything
that makes up the activity we call work is a gift from God.
Work is owned by God and lent to his creatures.

Second, the expectations of God are clear—he expects
service. The worker is a servant, actively working to produce

something for his or her master. Work is thus a duty imposed by God on his creatures. Laziness and inactivity are harshly judged. We might say that the goal is work at full capacity.

Third, work becomes the arena of creaturely choice. Once the stewards have been entrusted with their master's wealth, it is up to their choice and initiative to do something with it. Moral responsibility is a necessary part of work, once we grant the premise that the worker is a steward.

Furthermore, God judges his creatures on the basis of their service. Good servants are rewarded, though not with conventional standards of reward. By contrast, the unprofitable servant is banished from God's sight and the joyful community. What matters most is obviously what the master thinks about the service and work of his servants. The world's assessment of the servants' work is not even mentioned.

Finally, the parable of the talents reverses the customary view of the rewards of work. In the parable, the reward of the faithful stewards is the approval of their master. Financial rewards do not even enter the picture. Instead the master promises that because the workers "have been faithful over a little, I will set you over much" and he invites them to "enter into the joy of your master." This is obviously a picture of heavenly reward for those who have served God by their stewardship.

Some Practical Results of Viewing Work as a Stewardship

Several important ideas emerge from the principle that work is essentially a form of stewardship in which the worker serves God with the work that God provides. One is that work is a gift. God gives the materials for the worker and the very ability of the worker to perform the work. Gratitude for work is the natural response. To complain about a gift we have received has always been near the top of the list of ignominious behavior. Complaining about the gift of work is no exception.

The perspective of stewardship also affects our attitude toward the "ownership" of work. When work began to be viewed in primarily economic terms with the arrival of the industrial revolution, it became customary to look upon work as something the worker owns and sells to the highest bidder. As alternatives to that view, capitalism often operates on the premise that the employer owns the work of people (since work is a means of production), while socialism operates on the premise that society owns work. But the Christian view of the worker as steward suggests something truly revolutionary: God is the rightful owner of human work. There is a sense in which workers offer their work back to God.

The idea that work is a service to God also revolutionizes conventional attitudes about the goal or reward of work. Our whole cultural situation encourages us to think of our work as something we do for ourselves, our employer, or the public we serve. While we ask, "What's in it for me?" modern notions of accountability and job performance have also made us obsessed with pleasing the boss or the public. But where do we hear about pleasing God as the primary aim of work?

When we turn to the New Testament, we find an emphasis that sounds strange to modern ears:

> Whatever your task, work heartily, as serving the Lord and not men, knowing that from the Lord you will receive the inheritance as your reward; you are serving the Lord Christ (Colossians 3:23-24).

> Be obedient to those who are your earthly masters . . . as to Christ; not in the way of eyeservice, as men-pleasers, but as servants of Christ, doing the will of God from the heart, rendering service with a good will as to the Lord and not to men (Ephesians 6:5-7).

Our secular culture lacks the antennae by which to understand such a view of work, and I fear that Christians today find it just as foreign to their thinking.

It did not seem foreign to the original Protestants. Luther said that "the life of all Christians is intended for the eyes of God alone. . . . It is enough that our action is intended to satisfy and to glorify the One who sees it."[47] The same view is expressed in a poem a young Puritan wrote on the occasion of his twenty-third birthday. John Milton's seventh sonnet opens with self-rebuke at his lack of achievement to date. But the consolation expressed in the famous ending of the poem is based on the idea of work as stewardship to God:

> All is, if I have grace to use it so,
> As ever in my great task-master's eye.

The most plausible interpretation of the lines is this: "All that matters is that I have the grace to use my time in such a way that I am always conscious of living in my great taskmaster's presence." The evocative epithet "my great task-master" sums up the Puritan consciousness of working for God. The identity of the worker, in this view, comes from one's relationship to God, not from the prestige or financial rating of the job or task.

This fits in well with the distinctive contribution of Calvin to the history of work: he made the glory of God the goal of work. In the words of a modern historian,

> Calvin's contention was that a person's body . . . is not his own but is God's. Thus any talents he has in the performing of his work came not from himself but from God and should therefore be used for God's enhancement and not his own. All should be done to the glory of God. Work, then, should be discharged in this spirit of glorification, of duty, and of service to Him through service to fellow men.[48]

Here, in fact, is one of the antidotes to the syndrome of overwork that characterizes the contemporary work scene. It is hard to imagine God being glorified by the type of strain some people bring upon themselves as they pursue the advancement of their career or a lifestyle that requires overwork.

SUMMARY: A CHRISTIAN THEOLOGY OF WORK

The first Christian doctrine that underlies a Christian theology of work is creation. Made in the image of a God who himself works, people were created to work. As originally given by God to the human race, work was a blessing. It gave purpose to life, even in paradise.

When the human race fell, work became a curse. God himself imposed this quality on work as a punishment for human sin. As a result, we do not have to apologize for finding many of our tasks unpleasant or burdensome. Christianity takes a realistic approach to work.

But work can be redeemed from many of the effects of the fall. The key elements in that redemption are a realization that common work in the world bears God's approval, the belief that God calls us to our work, and an awareness that we are stewards who serve God with the work he has entrusted to us.

FURTHER READING

Alan Richardson, *The Biblical Doctrine of Work* (1952).

W. R. Forrester, *Christian Vocation* (1953).

Paul S. Minear, "Work and Vocation in Scripture," in *Work and Vocation: A Christian Discussion*, ed. John Oliver Nelson (1954).

Gustaf Wingren, *Luther on Vocation* (1957).

Wade H. Boggs, *All Ye Who Labor* (1962).

Carl F. H. Henry, *Aspects of Christian Social Ethics*, chapter 2 (1964).

Martin E. Clark, *Choosing Your Career* (1981).

In addition to these modern treatments, one of the best sources is the writings of the Puritans on work. Several key Puritan texts have been excerpted in modern anthologies:

John Cotton, *Christian Calling*, pp. 319-27 in vol. 1 of *The Puritans*, revised edition, ed. Perry Hiller and Thomas H. Johnson (1963).

Cotton Mather, *A Christian at His Calling*, pp. 122-27 in *Puritanism and the American Experience*, ed. Michael McGiffert (1969).

William Perkins, *A Treatise of the Vocations or Callings of Men*, pp. 35-59 in *Puritan Political Ideas, 1558-1794*, ed. Edmund S. Morgan (1965).

Chapter 5, Notes

1. Paul S. Minear, "Work and Vocation in Scripture," in *Work and Vocation: A Christian Discussion*, ed. John Oliver Nelson (New York: Harper and Brothers, 1954), 44.

2. Hesiod, *Works and Days*, as quoted by W. R. Forrester, *Christian Vocation* (New York: Charles Scribner's Sons, 1953), 121.

3. Forrester, 131.

4. Dorothy L. Sayers, "Why Work?" in *Creed or Chaos* (New York: Harcourt, Brace, 1949), 46, 53.

5. Alan Richardson, *The Biblical Doctrine of Work* (London: SCM, 1952), 21-22.

6. Wade H. Boggs, *All Ye Who Labor* (Richmond: John Knox Press, 1962), 13.

7. John Robinson, *Observations of Knowledge and Virtue*, as quoted in Richard Reinitz, ed., *Tensions in American Puritanism* (New York: John Wiley and Sons, 1970), 66.

8. J. M. Evans, *Paradise Lost and the Genesis Tradition* (Oxford: Oxford University Press, 1968), 249.

9. Milton, *Paradise Lost*, Book 4, lines 618-20.

10. For insightful commentary on this verse from Psalm 127, I commend the discussion of Minear, 40-44.

11. See the discussion by Gustaf Wingren, *Luther on Vocation*, trans. Carl C. Rasmussen (Philadelphia: Muhlenberg Press, 1957), 123ff.

12. Luther, exposition on Deuteronomy 8:17-18, as excerpted in *What Luther Says*, ed. Ewald M. Plass (St. Louis: Concordia Publishing House, 1959), 1495.

13. John Stott, "Reclaiming the Biblical Doctrine of Work," *Christianity Today*, 4 May 1979, 37.

14. Forrester, 130.

15. Ibid., 129.

16. Richardson, 36-37.

17. Ibid., 20-21.

18. Minear, 40-41.

19. Hugh Latimer, as quoted in H. M. Robertson, *Aspects of the Rise of Economic Individualism* (New York: Kelley and Millman, 1959), 10.

20. Richard Steele, *The Tradesman's Calling*, as quoted in R. H. Tawney, *Religion and the Rise of Capitalism* (New York: Harcourt, Brace, 1926), 245.

21. John Cotton, *Christian Calling*, in *The Puritans*, ed. Perry Miller and Thomas H. Johnson (New York: Harper, 1963), 1:319.

22. Wingren, 125.

23. Luther, sermon on Matthew 6:24-34, as excerpted in Plass, 560.

24. Luther, as quoted by Forrester, 147.

25. Forrester, 23.

26. Minear, 48-49.

27. William Perkins, *A Treatise of the Vocations or Callings of Men*, as excerpted in *Puritan Political Ideas, 1558-1794*, ed. Edmund S. Morgan (Indianapolis: Bobbs-Merrill, 1965), 59.

28. Karl Holl, "The History of the Word Vocation," *Review and Expositor* 55 (1958):126-54.

29. Holl, 153.

30. K. E. Kirk, *The Vision of God*, as quoted in Forrester, 35.

31. Boggs, 41-45.

32. John Calvin, *Institutes of the Christian Religion*, 3. 10. 6, trans. Henry Beveridge (Grand Rapids, Mich.: Wm. B. Eerdmans Publishing Co., 1972), 2:34.

33. Perkins, in Morgan, 36.

34. Calvin, commentary on 1 Corinthians 7:20, in *The First Epistle of Paul the Apostle to the Corinthians*, trans. John W. Fraser (Grand Rapids, Mich.: Wm. B. Eerdmans Publishing Co., 1960), 153.

35. Perkins, in Morgan, 37.

36. Luther, exposition of 1 Peter 2:18-20, in Plass, 1500-1501.

37. Cotton, in Miller and Johnson, 1:322.

38. Minear, 49.

39. Cotton, in Miller and Johnson, 1:322-23.

40. Cotton Mather, *A Christian at His Calling*, in *Puritanism and the American Experience*, ed. Michael McGiffert (Reading, Mass.: Addison-Wesley, 1969), 127.

41. Calvin, *First Corinthians*, 153.

42. Luther, sermon on 1 Peter 4:8-11, in Plass, 1497.

43. Mather, in McGiffert, 127.

44. Calvin, *Institutes*, 3. 10. 6.

45. Sayers, 59.

46. Lester De Koster, *Work: The Meaning of Your Life* (Grand Rapids, Mich.: Christian's Library Press, 1983), 39-43, has good commentary on the parable as it relates to the subject of work.

47. Luther, sermon on Matthew 6:16-18, in *Luther's Works*, ed. Jaroslav Pelikan and Helmut T. Lehmann (St. Louis: Concordia Publishing House, 1956), 21:164.

48. Robert S. Michaelsen, "Changes in the Puritan Concept of Calling or Vocation," *New England Quarterly* 26 (1953):317.

Chapter 6

The Ethics of Work

A Christian *theology* of work identifies the broad principles that influence how we think about work. The *ethics* of work focuses on the behavior of the worker, especially in relationship to other people or things. The ethics of work is concerned with the virtues and vices of workers, including both their actions and motives. As we explore the ethics of work, our main source will again be the Bible, supplemented by the comments of Christian thinkers who have interpreted the Bible helpfully.

The Bible is a rich source of practical advice about work. Someone has rightly observed that

> the Bible has . . . far more to say about daily chores than most of its readers realize. Indeed, we may think of it as an album of casual photographs of laborers. . . . A book by workers, about workers, for workers—that is the Bible.[1]

From the Bible we can assemble an ever-expanding picture of how God intends us to work.

WORK AS A MORAL DUTY

The Bible treats work as a moral duty laid upon the human race. Work was an expectation that God had for Adam and Eve both before and after the Fall. "Six days you shall labor, and do all your work," God commands in the fourth commandment (Exodus 20:9). Psalm 104, a nature psalm, places human work in the cycle of nature. Work is as natural as the rising of the sun:

> When the sun rises
> . . . .
> Man goes forth to his work
> and to his labor until the evening.
> (Psalm 104:22-23)

Other parts of the Bible likewise treat work as a duty and industriousness as a virtue. Paul enjoins Christians "to be ready for any honest work" (Titus 3:1). Nehemiah recalls that the wall of Jerusalem was rebuilt with dispatch because "the people had a mind to work" (Nehemiah 4:6). Industriousness is one of the chief traits of the virtuous wife described in Proverbs 31 (vv. 13-27), who emphatically "does not eat the bread of idleness" (v. 27). To the Thessalonians Paul commanded, "We exhort you . . . to work with your hands" (1 Thessalonians 4:10, 11).

Dispraise of Idleness

The most customary biblical way of asserting the moral duty of work is to denounce idleness or sloth. The Old Testament book of Proverbs can hardly stay away from the subject, as the following specimens suggest:

> Go to the ant, O sluggard;
> consider her ways, and be wise.
> Without having any chief,
> officer or ruler,
> she prepares her food in summer,
> and gathers her sustenance in harvest.

How long will you lie there, O sluggard?
    When will you arise from your sleep?
A little sleep, a little slumber,
    a little folding of the hands to rest,
and poverty will come upon you like a vagabond,
    and want like an armed man.
                    (Proverbs 6:6-11)

The soul of the sluggard craves, and gets nothing,
    while the soul of the diligent is richly supplied.
                    (Proverbs 13:4)

Slothfulness casts into a deep sleep,
    and an idle person will suffer hunger.
                    (Proverbs 19:15)

The desire of the sluggard kills him
    for his hands refuse to labor.
                    (Proverbs 21:25)

The common denominator of proverbs such as these is that to refuse to work conscientiously is to deny one's responsibility to oneself and to the human race.

Other parts of the Bible share this negative attitude toward laziness or sloppiness in work. We read, for example, that "through sloth the roof sinks in, / and through indolence the house leaks" (Ecclesiastes 10:18). Paul disparaged those who were "living in idleness, mere busybodies, not doing any work" (2 Thessalonians 3:11).

It has become common for writers in our day to debunk the original Protestants for praising the virtue of hard work. From a biblical perspective, it is the modern attitude, not the original Protestants, that needs correcting. As a Puritan wrote, "Religion does not seal warrants to idleness. . . . . God sets all his children to work. . . . God will bless our diligence, not our laziness."[2] It should strike us as an odd state of affairs that such an attitude needs defense today.

At its simplest, the morality of work is simply the duty to work. Within this framework, diligence in work is a virtue; sloth or laziness is a vice.

THE PURPOSES OF WORK

It is a principle of ethics that human conduct must be understood in terms of its purposes. These purposes sometimes allow us to judge whether an action is moral or immoral. Before we turn to work in its relationships, therefore, we need to consider the purposes of work.

At a human level, the primary purpose of work is to provide for human needs, both our own and those of others.[3] This is the context within which biblical writers praise work and denounce laziness.

On the positive side, we have comments such as these from wisdom literature:

> He who tills his land will have plenty of bread,
>> but he who follows worthless pursuits will have
>> plenty of poverty.
>> (Proverbs 28:19)

> A worker's appetite works for him;
>> his mouth urges him on.
>> (Proverbs 16:26)

Work is rooted in the necessity to provide for basic human needs. In the New Testament, Paul laid down the command for Christians to "work in quietness and to earn their own living" (2 Thessalonians 3:12).

This same view of work can be found in biblical passages that criticize slothfulness for its failure to provide for human needs. Thus "an idle person will suffer hunger" (Proverbs 19:15), and "the sluggard . . . will seek at harvest and have nothing" (Proverbs 20:4). Again, "Love not sleep, lest you come to poverty; / open your eyes, and you will have plenty of bread" (Proverbs 20:13).

At this level, work quite obviously rests on a utilitarian ethic. It is commendable because it is useful to oneself and society in providing for the basic needs of life. Such a work ethic does not find a place for work done to feed extravagance or ostentatious consumption. It also brings into question a leading feature of our own consumer-oriented economy—the manufacture and consumption of goods and services that people do not really need. In fact, much of our advertising is based on the practice of inducing people to buy things they do not need.

I am reminded of comments made by two well-known British Christians of this century. In a discussion of Christian ethics, C. S. Lewis paints a brief picture of what the Christian society outlined in the New Testament would look like if put into practice. Part of the picture is this:

> There are to be no passengers or parasites: if man does not work, he ought not to eat. Every one is to work with his own hands, and what is more, every one's work is to produce something good: there will be no manufacture of silly luxuries, and then of sillier advertisements to persuade us to buy them.[4]

Dorothy Sayers paints a much grimmer picture of the consumer society into which Western civilization has fallen in the twentieth century.[5] "The gluttonous consumption of manufactured goods," she writes, has become "the prime civic virtue." It has resulted in a "vicious circle of production and consumption." Accompanying ills include a "furious barrage of advertisement by which people are flattered into a greedy hankering after goods which they do not really need," a decline in the quality of goods ("you must not buy goods that last too long, for production cannot be kept going unless the goods wear out, or fall out of fashion, and so can be thrown away and replaced with others"), and designing work in such a way that it does not engage the interest of the worker, lest the worker "desire to make a thing as well as it can be made, and that would not pay." Sayers' final conclusion has a prophetic ring: "The sin of Gluttony, of Greed, of overmuch stuffing of ourselves, is the sin that has delivered us over into the power of the machine."

Both Lewis and Sayers alert us to the fact that there is a vast difference between work based on a utilitarian ethic and work based on a consumer ethic. At a personal level, it would seem that Christian workers should ask the question of the usefulness of the work they do. Harold Lehman has written that "any work in which a contribution can be made somewhere to the total needs of man must be regarded as a good and natural way for a Christian to live in his calling."[6] The reverse side of this principle is that if a person's work does not contribute to the needs of society, it is not fulfilling its God-intended purpose.

A second purpose of work is to provide meaning and self-fulfillment for human life. The Bible does not state this directly, but it follows logically from the fact that God, who himself is a creative worker, made people in his image and gave them work to do. God gave Adam and Eve dominion over the world (Genesis 1:26, 28). Work was creative; it declared the creature's humanity.

This ideal remains the goal for work, even though work in a fallen world often falls short of that purpose. Judged by this purpose, work is moral when it leads to human fulfillment. By the same standard, work becomes immoral when it dehumanizes the worker, since such work does not meet God's intention for work. John Stott has written,

> Our potential for creative work is an essential part
> of our Godlike humanness, and without work we
> are not fully human. If we are idle (instead of busy)
> or destructive (instead of creative) we deny our humanity and so forfeit our self-fulfillment.[7]

In our consumer-oriented society, the tendency is overwhelming to act on the premise that work is acceptable if it produces what society wants. The result, as we know, is an abundance of jobs that are uncreative and dehumanizing. If we gave priority to the principle that work should be as fulfilling as possible, instead of giving priority to the human appetite for goods, we would eliminate many jobs and the goods or services they produce. From the viewpoint of Christian ethics, this would be a step in the right direction.

In addition to the purposes of providing for human needs and human fulfillment, work has as its purpose the glory of God. God's own work glorifies him as creator. Furthermore, God is the one who calls people to their tasks. To accept those tasks is to obey God and thus bring glory to him. Stated as an ethical principle, any work performed in a moral way for a moral purpose pleases God. Of course the perversion of work remains a possibility. People can carry out their work with no thought of God as the one who calls them to it, and they can perform their work in an immoral way.

It goes without saying that work done in an immoral way or in the service of immoral activities does not glorify God. Within the Bible we find examples of trade based on idolatry (Acts 19:19-27), exploitation (numerous prophetic passages), or dishonesty (Luke 3:12-14). In our day, the decline in morality in society at large has greatly amplified the incidence of work based in immorality. Examples include the practice of deceiving people into paying for unnecessary work, cheating either management or the consumer, dishonest business practices, and work related to such immoral practices as pornography or drunkenness.

Summary

Work serves three main purposes in the world. It exists to provide for human needs, to fulfill our humanity, and to glorify God. These goals, in turn, are standards by which we can weigh the morality of work. Work that satisfies these purposes is moral in nature. Some work, of course, fails to measure up to these ethical standards.

WORK IN RELATION TO ONESELF

I said earlier that the ethics of work is especially concerned with the worker's relationships. The logical starting place is to consider work in relation to the worker.

Several factors have conspired to make us feel guilty when we think that work exists for the fulfillment and pleasure of the worker. We know that work is often a curse. Christians, moreover, operate on the premise that the ultimate purpose of their work is not something selfish but something at least potentially sacrificial in the service of God and humanity.

But in a Christian view we do not need to apologize for finding enjoyment and fulfillment in work. Jesus commanded people to love their neighbor *as they love themselves* [italics mine] (Matthew 22:39). God does not call workers to be masochists. In fact, the Bible has plenty to say about the rewards that should come to workers. God intends work to be a joy, not a pain we inflict on ourselves.

There is a legitimate satisfaction that workers can take in the provision they earn by their work. Psalm 128 begins with this pronouncement of blessing:

> Blessed is every one who fears the LORD,
>   who walks in his ways!
> You shall eat the fruit of the labor of your hands;
>   you shall be happy, and it shall be well with you.

The poet's wish for the virtuous wife is, "Give her of the fruit of her hands" (Proverbs 31:31). To enjoy the benefits of what one has worked for is one of the moral pleasures of life.

Nor does the Bible frown on the idea of working in order to be prosperous and successful. Here are some variations on this theme:

> A slack hand causes poverty,
>   but the hand of the diligent makes rich.
> (Proverbs 10:4)

The hand of the diligent will rule,
  while the slothful will be put to forced labor.
                                   (Proverbs 12:24)

The soul of the sluggard craves, and gets nothing,
  while the soul of the diligent is richly supplied.
                                   (Proverbs 13:4)

The plans of the diligent lead surely to abundance,
  but every one who is hasty comes only to want.
                                   (Proverbs 21:5)

Do you see a man skilful [KJV, diligent] in his work?
  he will stand before kings;
  he will not stand before obscure men.
                                   (Proverbs 22:29)

The Bible is hostile to the success ethic in which people worship success, but it does not disparage the legitimate satisfaction that workers take in being successful in their work, or in the material prosperity that might come from such success. There is nothing immoral about working to have a successful career, though such a career must, of course, not be gained at the expense of other moral concerns. Biblical heroes such as Joseph and Daniel had astoundingly successful careers, to the glory of God and the benefit of society. Paul was the world's most successful missionary.

Joy in one's work is another attitude the Bible encourages. The God-centered passages in the book of Ecclesiastes are filled with exuberance over the worker's delight in his or her work:

There is nothing better for a man than that he should eat and drink and find enjoyment in his toil. This also, I saw, is from the hand of God (Ecclesiastes 2:24).

It is God's gift to man that every one should eat and drink and take pleasure in all his toil (Ecclesiastes 3:13).

Sweet is the sleep of a laborer (Ecclesiastes 5:12).

Behold what I have seen to be good and to be fitting
is to eat and drink and find enjoyment in all the toil
with which one toils. . . . Every man also to whom
God has given wealth and possessions and power
to enjoy them, and to accept his lot and find enjoyment in his toil—this is the gift of God (Ecclesiastes
5:18-19).

Work at its best is personally fulfilling. Not all of our
tasks, of course, measure up to this ideal. But when they do,
we should accept the joy they bring with gratitude. Dorothy
Sayers has written that

work is not, primarily, a thing one does to live, but
the thing one lives to do. It is, or it should be, the
full expression of the worker's faculties, the thing
in which he finds spiritual, mental, and bodily satisfaction, and the medium in which he offers himself
to God.[8]

This is the moral goal of work in the life of the worker.

WORK IN RELATION TO SOCIETY

The morality of work also involves the relationship between work and society. Work occurs in a social context. The
work we do nearly always brings us into contact with other
people. As someone has written, work "joins us to the community of fellow workers. . . . Work remains . . . the expression
of a unique human connectedness—a gift each human gives
to every other human and each generation gives to the next."[9]

To begin, the work we do to provide for our own needs
is something we owe to society. The Bible takes a very negative
view toward social parasites who refuse to support themselves.
The best known passage on the subject is 2 Thessalonians 3:10-
12:

> For even when we were with you, we gave you this
> command: If any one will not work, let him not eat.
> For we hear that some of you are living in idleness,
> mere busybodies, not doing any work. Now such
> persons we command and exhort in the Lord Jesus
> Christ to do their work in quietness and to earn their
> own living.

Paul himself declined to accept payment for his work as a
missionary, choosing instead to work "night and day, that we
might not burden any of you" (1 Thessalonians 2:9).

The duty people have to work for their own livelihood
extends to their families as well as themselves. Paul wrote to
Timothy that "if any one does not provide for his relatives,
and especially for his own family, he has disowned the faith
and is worse than an unbeliever" (1 Timothy 5:8).

As that statement suggests, for Christians there is an
element of witness in the work they perform. After all, the
world looks on as we work or fail to work, whether on the
job or around the house. This too is part of the communal
dimension of work. Again Paul is the leading biblical source:

> We exhort you . . . to work with your hands, as we
> charged you; so that you may command the respect
> of outsiders, and be dependent on nobody (1 Thes-
> salonians 4:10, 11).

Elsewhere Paul claims that the Christian's work itself serves
as a model for others to follow:

> For you yourselves know how you ought to imitate
> us; we were not idle when we were with you, we
> did not eat any one's bread without paying, but with
> toil and labor we worked night and day, that we
> might not burden any of you. It was not because
> we have not that right, but to give you in our conduct
> an example to imitate (2 Thessalonians 3:7-9).

Yet another way in which our work relates us to society is that the profits we reap from our work enable us to extend our generosity to people in need. This is the picture that emerges, for example, from the portrait of the industrious wife in Proverbs 31. This human dynamo works almost nonstop, not only for herself and her family, but she also "opens her hand to the poor, and reaches out her hands to the needy" (Proverbs 31:20). The apostle Paul put it into the form of a command: "Let the thief no longer steal, but rather let him labor, doing honest work with his hands, so that he may be able to give to those in need" (Ephesians 4:28).

The social dimension of work keeps expanding, reaching out to include not being a burden to society, providing a witness to society, and extending compassion to society. But the biggest idea of all is that work is a way of serving humanity. Support for this ideal comes mainly from the Puritans, but the principle appears in the Bible as well.

At the heart of the Christian faith is the idea that we are called to be servants. "Whoever would be great among you," Jesus told his disciples, "must be your servant, and whoever would be first among you must be your slave; even as the Son of man came not to be served but to serve" (Matthew 20:26-28). On the basis of the example of Christ, Paul wrote,

> Let each of you look not only to his own interests,
> but also to the interests of others. Have this mind
> among yourselves, which is yours in Christ Jesus,
> who . . . [took] the form of a servant (Philippians
> 2:4-5, 7).

The practice of service is the heart of Christian morality. Applied to work, it means that an element of self-sacrifice is a necessary part of our work.

To view work as a form of service to humanity redeems almost any task that is in itself unrewarding. It is the great balancing factor to that work which carries its own reward and which we find inherently satisfying. Much of the work we do does not rise to that ideal. We conduct our work between the poles of self-fulfillment and service toward others. To view ourselves as serving others can give such work a moral purpose and a reason for us to be satisfied in doing it. If at any point in our lives we are involved in work that we cannot defend as being a genuine service to others, we should look for other work.

John Stott once received a letter from the chief health inspector of the Port of London. Work for his own ends did not satisfy him. But he went on to say, "I like to think that I am responsible for a part of the greater field pattern whereby all serve human welfare and obey the will of our wonderful Creator."[10]

The people who said the most on the subject were the original Protestants. I should note in passing that I look in vain for comments from them attesting that personal prosperity is the goal of work, the attitude with which "the Protestant ethic" is often charged.

Even the Reformation view of callings was rooted in the idea of service. "All stations," wrote Luther, "are so oriented that they serve others."[11] Luther denounced people who "do not use their talents in their calling or in the service of their neighbor; they use them only for their own glory and advantage."[12]

The theme of work as service to humanity was a virtual obsession with the Puritans. "God hath made man a sociable creature," wrote Cotton Mather; "we are beneficial to human society by the works of that special occupation in which we are to be employed, according to the order of God."[13] One of the reasons the Protestants denied that Catholic monks had a legitimate calling is that their life did not serve society.

To view work as service to others should, said the Puritans, govern one's choice of a vocation. Richard Baxter wrote, "Choose not that [calling] in which you may be most rich or honorable in the world; but that in which you may do most good."[14] The same ethical outlook affects how one pursues his or her work after entering a vocation. Baxter, for example, enjoined lawyers to be more interested in promoting justice than making money, and physicians to "be sure that the saving of men's lives and health be first and chiefly your intention before any gain or honor of your own."[15]

The most complete Puritan discussion of this matter is by William Perkins.[16] "The main end of our lives," he writes, "is to serve God in the serving of men in the works of our callings." God could, if he chose, preserve people "without the help of men, but his pleasure is that men should be his instruments for the good of one another." "By this we learn," adds Perkins, "how men of mean [humble] place and calling may comfort themselves. Let them consider that in serving of men . . . they serve God . . . and though their reward from men be little, yet the reward at God's hand shall not be wanting. . . . And thus may we reap marvelous [contentment] in any kind of calling, though it be but to sweep the house or keep sheep."

There can be little doubt that one of the problems with work in our day is an overly individualistic work ethic. People overwhelmingly accept the duty of work, if they accept it at all, in a spirit of asking, What's in it for me? To view work as service to society introduces a moral perspective that is at odds with the prevailing ethic.

To stress work as service to others does not, of course, cancel what was said earlier about working to meet our own needs. We can follow the lead of the Puritans in being realistic and balanced on this score. A worker must be diligent in his or her calling, claimed Mather, "so he may glorify God, by doing of good for others and getting of good for himself."[17] The same balance is present in the formulation of Perkins:

> Some man will say perchance: What, must we not labor in our callings to maintain our families? I answer: this must be done: but this is not the scope and end of our lives. The true end of our lives is to do service to God in serving of man.[18]

WORK IN RELATION TO GOD

A third relationship that work entails is the relationship between the worker and God. This relationship is rooted in God's calling of people to their tasks and occupations. When we work with this sense of vocation, we do our work in a spirit of faith and obedience. This too makes work moral.

Viewing work as something God entrusts to us as stewards also carries with it a set of moral attitudes. If it is true that finding enjoyment in our work "is from the hand of God" (Ecclesiastes 2:24), gratitude and a spirit of thanksgiving become proper attitudes for the worker. The same doctrine of stewardship offers a new motivation for doing work, which is done ultimately "as to the Lord and not to men" (Ephesians 6:7).

The same Godward view of work affects how we enter a vocation or decide what tasks to undertake. If work is something to which God calls us, we have every reason to listen to his call. This, in turn, prompts us to other considerations than the common criterion of financial reward. The topic of choosing a career is beyond the scope of this book and is a topic already much discussed.[19] But let me note in passing that if we believe our work is something that relates us to God as stewards, we will choose careers and tasks on the basis of such considerations as the degree to which those careers utilize the talents and abilities God has given us, allow for maximum achievement (and therefore represent a good stewardship of our time as well as of our abilities), and provide the greatest potential for witness (on the job, through our work, and as an outgrowth of our work).

THE WORKER'S RELATIONSHIP TO WORK

A final relationship is the worker in relation to work. Because work itself is not a person, it is easy to overlook it as an ingredient in the morality of work. Yet the worker's relationship to it at once makes it a moral issue.

Commitment to excellence in work is one of the prime

moral virtues the Bible prescribes for workers. Excellence is a Christian ideal for all of life. Christians are called to excellence because the God they serve is excellent.[20] It is an ideal that is bigger than work, but it includes work also.

The work of God himself is "very good" (Genesis 1:31). The work of his human creatures should aspire to the same quality. Paul's command to Timothy about the work of preaching states a principle that applies to work more generally: "Do your best to present yourself to God as one approved, a workman who has no need to be ashamed" (2 Timothy 2:15).

The Christian writer who in our century has written best on the subject of the Christian's commitment to excellence in work is Dorothy Sayers.[21] She begins by rejecting the commonly accepted notion that a person's life "is divided into the time he spends on his work and the time he spends in serving God." The ideal is for a Christian "to serve God in his work, and the work itself must be accepted and respected as the medium of divine creation." This requires a belief that work itself has integrity. No degree of piety in the worker, writes Sayers, "will compensate for work that is not true to itself; for any work that is untrue to its own technique is a living lie." Sayers believes that the church in our century

> has forgotten that the secular vocation is sacred. Forgotten that a building must be good architecture before it can be a good church; that a painting must be well painted before it can be a good sacred picture; that work must be good work before it can call itself God's work.

"The only Christian work," concludes Sayers, "is good work well done. . . . The worker's first duty is to *serve the work*."

A second moral stance of a worker to his or her work is that work should be done with zest. One of the memorable proverbs about work is this one: "Whatever your hand finds to do, do it with your might" (Ecclesiastes 9:10). A New Testament epistle urges a similar attitude: "Whatever your task, work heartily, as serving the Lord and not men" (Colossians 3:23). The implied vice is to be half-hearted in one's work.

A third attitude we should bring to our work is to avoid making an idol of it. An idol is anything people elevate to the place of supremacy that only God should have in their life. Everyone elevates something to a position of supremacy. Claus Westermann, in the conclusion to his book *The Praise of God in the Psalms*, writes, "Exalting is part of existence. It is so much a part of it, that when one has ceased to exalt God, something else must be exalted. . . . Exalting remains a function of existence."[22] Chad Walsh, in a book on utopian literature, voices a similar viewpoint:

> Man is incurably religious. . . . If one thinks of religion as the ultimate concern, most men have it. The American who does not worship an authentic God is almost certain to have a substitute deity: The American Way of Life, Free Enterprise, the Standard of Living, the arts—or sex—at least something. Whatever his deity, he offers sacrifices to it, whether he is the young executive conforming to the expectations of his superiors or the young artist half starving in the service of his Muse. . . . The Bible devotes remarkably little time to the menace of atheism. The biblical viewpoint seems to be that atheism is a rare and puny adversary compared to idolatry.[23]

The workaholics I discussed in an earlier chapter have made work their religion. One article called them "the new Calvinists."[24] "Work is the religion of the young and ambitious," notes the article about these people who forego personal relationships as they work seventy hours per week. "You shall have no other gods before me," says the first of the Ten Commandments (Exodus 20:3). Work is one of these forbidden gods.

This leads naturally to a final strand in a worker's moral stance toward his or her work—the principle of moderation. The moral ideal of a golden mean between extremes belongs

to the wisdom of the human race, having been first established
in Western consciousness by the Greek philosopher Aristotle.
It is also a biblical standard. The following proverb applies the
principle to the realm of work and economics:

> give me neither poverty nor riches;
> feed me with the food that is needful for me
> (Proverbs 30:8).

Moderation in work means avoiding the extremes of laziness and overwork. We have already noted the biblical and
Puritan prohibition against slothfulness in work. The more
likely abuse in our society is overwork.

The original Protestants warned against it, and their cautions remain valid. The Scottish divine Robert Woodrow commented, "The sin of our too great fondness for trade, to the
neglecting of our more valuable interests, I humbly think will
be written upon our judgment."[25] The Puritan Phillip Stubbes
claimed that workers should not allow "immoderate care" to
"surpass the bounds of . . . true godliness,"[26] while Luther
cautioned that "a person should work in such a way that he
remains well and does no injury to his body."[27] In a culture
that worships economic and vocational success, the danger of
immoderate work is a constant moral temptation.

SUMMARY

To unify what we have said about the morality of work,
let me offer as a summarizing principle that the worker is more
important than the work. The Bible says a great deal more
about the attitudes of the worker than about work. Someone
who made a study of the matter concluded,

> Throughout the Bible it is the person who works to
> whom most attention is given, rather than the form
> or conditions of his work. . . . Biblical writers [em-
> phasize] the agent more than the act, the motive of
> the laborer more than the mode of his labor.[28]

It is not so much work that is moral or immoral, but the worker. What things, then, characterize the moral worker? The moral worker accepts the duty of work as a means of providing for human needs, of finding purpose in life, and of glorifying God. The moral worker attempts to find legitimate self-satisfaction in work, to serve society through his or her work, and to view work as a medium for living a life of faith before God. In regard to work itself, the moral worker is committed to excellence and to moderation.

In view of the emphasis we have placed on the worker and his relationships, it is appropriate to conclude this chapter with an account of a brief interchange in a medieval stone masons' yard. "What are you doing?" a visitor asked the first stone mason. "I'm cutting a stone," the mason replied. A second stone mason replied, "I'm earning my living." A third stone mason responded, "I'm building a cathedral." As these responses suggest, our attitude toward our work is what matters most.

FURTHER READING

Dorothy L. Sayers, "Why Work?" in *Creed or Chaos?* (1949).
Paul S. Minear, "Work and Vocation in Scripture," in *Work and Vocation: A Christian Discussion*, ed. John Oliver Nelson, pp. 32-81 (1954).
Arthur F. Holmes, *Contours of a World View*, chapter 14 (1983).

Chapter 6, Notes

1. Paul S. Minear, "Work and Vocation in Scripture," in *Work and Vocation: A Christian Discussion*, ed. John Oliver Nelson (New York: Harper and Brothers, 1954), 33.

2. Thomas Watson, *The Beatitudes* (Edinburgh: Banner of Truth Trust, 1971), 257.

3. I borrow the idea from Arthur F. Holmes, *Contours of a World View* (Grand Rapids, Mich.: Wm. B. Eerdmans Publishing Co., 1983), 219.

4. C. S. Lewis, *Mere Christianity* (New York: Macmillan Publishing Co., 1943, 1960), 80.

5. Dorothy L. Sayers, *Creed or Chaos?* (New York: Harcourt, Brace, 1949), 69-70.

6. Harold D. Lehman, *In Praise of Leisure* (Scottdale, Penn.: Herald Press, 1974), 117.

7. John Stott, "Reclaiming the Biblical Doctrine of Work," *Christianity Today*, 4 May 1979, 36.

8. Sayers, p. 53.

9. John C. Raines and Donna C. Day-Lower, *Modern Work and Human Meaning* (Philadelphia: Westminster Press, 1986), 16-17.

10. Stott, 37.

11. Luther, as quoted in Gustaf Wingren, *Luther on Vocation*, trans. Carl C. Rasmussen (Philadelphia: Muhlenberg Press, 1957), 5.

12. Luther, sermon on 1 Peter 4:8-11, as excerpted in *What Luther Says: An Anthology*, ed. Ewald M. Plass (St. Louis: Concordia Publishing House, 1959), 1497.

13. Cotton Mather, *A Christian at His Calling*, in *Puritanism and the American Experience*, ed. Michael McGiffert (Reading, Mass.: Addison-Wesley, 1969), 122.

14. Richard Baxter, *A Christian Directory*, as quoted in A. M. Robertson, *Aspects of the Rise of Economic Individualism* (New York: Kelley and Millman, 1959), 16.

15. Baxter, as quoted in Winthrop S. Hudson, "Puritanism and the Spirit of Capitalism," in *Protestantism and Capitalism: The Weber Thesis and Its Critics*, ed. Robert W. Green (Boston: D. C. Heath, 1959), 59.

16. William Perkins, *A Treatise of the Vocations or Callings of Men*, in *Puritan Political Ideas, 1558-1794*, ed. Edmund S. Morgan (Indianapolis: Bobbs-Merrill, 1965), especially 56-57.

17. Cotton Mather, *Two Brief Discourses*, as quoted in Ralph Barton Perry, *Puritanism and Democracy* (New York: Vanguard, 1944), 312.

18. Perkins, in Morgan, 56-57.

19. Good discussions on choosing a career include these books: Jerry and Mary White, *Your Job: Survival or Satisfaction?* (Grand Rapids, Mich.: Zondervan Publishing House, 1977); Martin E. Clark, *Choosing Your Career* (Phillipsburg, N.J.: Presbyterian and Reformed Publishing Co., 1981); Pamela Moran, *The Christian Job Hunter* (Ann Arbor: Servant Books, 1984). There are also some mediocre and unhelpful books on the subject.

20. See Frank E. Gaebelein's essay "The Idea of Excellence and Our Obligation to It," in *The Christian, The Arts, and Truth*, ed. D. Bruce Lockerbie (Portland, Ore.: Multnomah Press, 1985), 141- 49.

21. Sayers, 56-60.

22. Claus Westermann, *Praise and Lament in the Psalms*, trans. Keith R. Crim (Atlanta: John Knox Press, 1981), 160.

23. Chad Walsh, *From Utopia to Nightmare* (New York: Harper and Row, 1962), 143-44.

24. Richard Phillips, "The New Calvinists," *Chicago Tribune*, 5 November 1986, sec. 7, pp. 5-8.

25. Robert Woodrow, quoted in R. H. Tawney, *Religion and the Rise of Capitalism* (New York: Harcourt, Brace, 1926), 238.

26. Phillip Stubbes, *Anatomy of the Abuses in England*, as quoted in Tawney, 216.

27. Luther, sermon on Mark 8:1-9, in Plass, 1496-97.

28. Minear, 40-41.

29. Mather, *Christian at His Calling*, 124.

Chapter 7

A Christian Theology of Leisure

A s we turn to a consideration of leisure from a Christian perspective, it will be helpful to review some of the foundational ideas about leisure discussed at the beginning of this book. At its most rudimentary, leisure is time free from the constraints of work and other obligations of living. The word itself implies cessation from work. In its higher reaches, leisure takes on additional overtones of human freedom to cultivate an enriched state of being.

The rewards of leisure include rest from work, celebration, enjoyment, establishing personal meaning and identity, and fostering social relationships. When put into a context of traditional ethical viewpoints, leisure is incompatible with idleness, utilitarianism, and self-abasement. Conversely, it flourishes when people believe that pleasure and human fulfillment are good.

The purpose of this chapter is to examine how these ideas about leisure fare when placed alongside the relevant Christian doctrines. I should note that when I came to integrate ideas about leisure with the relevant Christian doctrines, I felt I was working in something of a vacuum. There are plenty of books that claim to provide a Christian theology of leisure, but except for Robert K. Johnston's *The Christian at Play* , I found them notably vague and insubstantial, with almost no attempt to root an author's personal (and sometimes fanciful) opinions in the Bible.

REST AS A CREATION ORDINANCE

It is common knowledge that God established work as a creation ordinance. It is not so well known that rest from work is equally a creation ordinance.

The Rest of God

In an earlier chapter we traced work back to the work of God. We can do the same for leisure. Some theologians claim that the activity of God in creating the world was play. I cannot agree. The Bible calls it work. But in Genesis 1 God rested as well as worked. After each day of creation he contemplated and (we can infer) enjoyed what he had created, pronouncing it "good."

After the individual days of creation, each punctuated by rest, there came the grand finale—a whole day of rest. Here is how the Bible describes it:

> Thus the heavens and the earth were finished, and all the host of them. And on the seventh day God finished his work which he had done, and he rested on the seventh day from all his work which he had done. So God blessed the seventh day and hallowed it, because on it God rested from all his work which he had done in creation (Genesis 2:1-3).

What are we to make of the mystery of God's setting aside a day for rest? Later in history it became the model and sanction for setting aside a day to worship God. But we should not too hastily conclude that this was its meaning at the very beginning. Certainly God did not worship on the seventh day.

The Genesis account itself simply stresses the idea of cessation from labor.

The truth is that the exact origins of the Old Testament sabbath are veiled in mystery. Setting aside one day in seven as a religious day is at least as old as the exodus from Egypt (see Exodus 16), but it is not clear whether it stretches backward beyond that point. Some theologians believe that "originally the Sabbath was characterized merely by the prohibition of all work."[1]

We do not, of course, have to choose *between* rest and worship in our interpretation of the rest of God on the seventh day. One of the things that became apparent to me early in my work on this book is that a Christian view of leisure must incorporate the experience of worship. Leisure and worship have important things in common; we must regard worship as a particular kind of leisure. One thing worship and leisure have in common is cessation from work.

What, then, does God's rest from work say about leisure? It affirms leisure by drawing a boundary to human work and acquisitiveness. Like God's rest, leisure frees us from the need for productivity and allows us instead to enjoy what has already been made. It has within it the quality of "letting go" of the utilitarian urges that occupy us in the world of getting and spending. Josef Pieper is thus right in saying that leisure is the possession "of those who are open to everything; not of those who grab and grab hold, but of those who leave the reins loose. . . . almost like a man falling asleep."[2] There is an element of celebration of what has been accomplished in such rest.

Another thing we can infer from the rest of God after creation is that it was more than emptiness or idleness. Such rest has the positive quality of joy and satisfaction. It is linked, moreover, with contemplation, specifically of nature, artistry, and beauty. Having completed his work of creation, God "saw everything that he had made, and behold, it was very good" (Genesis 1:31). It would of course be arbitrary to say that this is the extent of what our leisure should consist of, but at the very least it sanctions contemplative and aesthetic uses of leisure. We might also note in passing that even in a technological age, leisure remains a prime means by which people renew their contact with nature.

There is, finally, a note of refreshment or re-creation in the rest of God. We learn this from Exodus 31:17, where sabbath observance is said to be "a sign for ever between me and the people of Israel that in six days the LORD made heaven and earth, and on the seventh day he rested, and was refreshed." Here the rest of God is defined, not by its activity, but by its function of refreshment, and in this, too, we can see a divine model for human rest and leisure.

Rest as a Commandment

The model of God's rest from work became a requirement for the human race in the Ten Commandments. Part of the fourth commandment is this:

> Remember the sabbath day, to keep it holy. Six days you shall labor, and do all your work; but the seventh day is a sabbath to the LORD your God; in it you shall not do any work . . . for in six days the LORD made heaven and earth, the sea, and all that is in them, and rested the seventh day; therefore the LORD blessed the sabbath day and hallowed it (Exodus 20:8-11).

Here the sabbath has become a holy day of worship while retaining the idea of resting and ceasing from work. As elaborated in the Mosaic ceremonial laws, the sabbath command shows clearly that God has prescribed times when people make a complete halt to utilitarian activities. God does not intend human life to be totally governed by utilitarian ends.

Another thing the fourth commandment suggests is that God's pattern for human life is a rhythm between work and rest. Neither work nor leisure is complete in itself. Each takes its meaning from the other. In prescribing a day of rest, the fourth commandment also commands us to work. Here is the integration of work and play in a harmonious cycle that is essential to a Christian view of leisure.

Other biblical passages reinforce the idea of God's provision for human rest from work. The annual feasts of the Old Testament calendar were days away from work. For example, on the first and seventh days of the feast of unleavened bread, as well as the day of first fruits, the Israelites were commanded to "do no laborious work" (Numbers 28:18, 25, 26). When the Israelites entered the promised land, they were commanded not to till their land and vineyards in the seventh and fiftieth years (Leviticus 25).

It is evident, then, how profoundly the idea of rest was embedded in the Hebrew consciousness. We can catch the refrain of this consciousness in a passage from the New Testament book of Hebrews (elaborated on in Richard Baxter's devotional classic *The Saints' Everlasting Rest*):

> So then, there remains a sabbath rest for the people of God; for whoever enters God's rest also ceases from his labors as God did from his.
>
> Let us therefore strive to enter that rest (Hebrews 4:9-11).

The Example of Jesus

To the Old Testament emphasis on the need for people to punctuate their active lives with rest, we can add the example of Jesus. Throughout his extraordinarily busy public years, Jesus found times of retreat. Here is a typical scenario:

> Immediately he made his disciples get into the boat and go before him to the other side, to Bethsaida, while he dismissed the crowd. And after he had taken leave of them, he went up on the mountain to pray. And when evening came, the boat was out on the sea, and he was alone on the land (Mark 6:45-47).

The Gospel of Luke gives us similar pictures of Jesus going to the mountains to pray (Luke 6:12; 9:28).

Jesus prescribed the same pattern for his disciples, as we see from an incident in the Gospel of Mark:

> The apostles returned to Jesus, and told him all that they had done and taught. And he said to them, "Come away by yourselves to a lonely place, and rest a while." For many were coming and going, and they had no leisure even to eat. And they went away in the boat to a lonely place by themselves (Mark 6:30-32).

These passages from the Gospels are important to our understanding of leisure. They show that Jesus did not reduce life to ceaseless evangelism. God draws a boundary to every type of work, even the work of proclaiming the gospel and helping people in their physical needs.

The event that makes the point most memorably is the story of Mary and Martha (Luke 10:38-42). The story features contrasting personality types—types that psychologists today call Type A and Type B. Martha is the activist, preoccupied with the work that needs to be done in order to get a meal on the table. Jesus criticizes her spirit as one that is "anxious and troubled about many things." Mary, by contrast, chose to retire, at least temporarily, from the obligations of work. Jesus commended her for having "chosen the good portion."

Summary

One of the theological bases of leisure is the principle of rest that God has implanted in the order of creation. Rest from labor emerges from the Bible as a human requirement.

When we read in the Bible that God commands people to work, we do not hesitate to consider that work as a calling from God. But God also calls us to rest. Rest, no less than work, is a calling from God.

Rest is a prerequisite for leisure and an ingredient of leisure, but it does not by itself constitute leisure. Leisure is activity and a quality of life, not mere cessation from work. Idleness is not leisure. We might say, then, that the biblical principle of rest provides a space within which leisure can occur.

THE VALUE OF THE NONUTILITARIAN

A second theological principle that underlies a Christian view of leisure is that nonutilitarian activities have value. In the opening chapter we noted that one of the identifying traits of leisure is that it is nonproductive in the sense in which we ordinarily use that term. Leisure does not meet our needs of physical or economic survival. It does not put bread on the table or clothes in the closet. Leisure is a self-enclosed world that carries its own reward:

> [Play] has many biological, psychological, and cultural values. . . . Yet . . . the purpose of play is in the play itself. If a person enters play only with useful, instrumental goals in mind, the activity ceases to be play. The most distinctive characteristic is that it is voluntary, spontaneous, a source of joy and amusement, an activity pursued exuberantly and fervently for its own sake.[3]

I am convinced that the biggest obstacle to leisure in modern times and in the Christian world is a prevailing utilitarian ethic. To be worthwhile, says this philosophy, something must be directly useful. If leisure and play are smuggled into such a world view at all, it is under the utilitarian banner: play can be tolerated because it makes work possible. What does the Bible say about such a utilitarian ethic?

God's Nonutilitarian Creation

Once again we can start with the creation account in early Genesis. God did not create a purely utilitarian world. He created a world in which much exists for the sake of beauty and delight. From a utilitarian viewpoint, God did not have to create a world filled with colors and symmetrical forms. He could have made everything a drab gray. He could have made trees whose leaves do not turn color in the fall or a world in which all flowers are brown or the grass is gray. At the heart of God's creation is something extravagant and gratuitous, going beyond what is strictly needed for survival. Someone has commented that the lilies Jesus told us to contemplate "are lazy lilies, occupying space amid the common field grasses for no reason other than that it pleases God. Can we appreciate God's creative prodigality?"[4] God made provision for the quality of human life, not simply its survival. He is the God who came that people "may have life, and have it abundantly" (John 10:10). At its best, leisure is part of the human quest for the abundant life.

God's Prescription of Nonutilitarianism

Just as God created a world that contains more than what is useful, he infused the same quality of nonutilitarianism into human life. The garden that God planted for Adam and Eve was not only utilitarian. We read that "out of the ground the LORD God made to grow every tree that is pleasant to the sight and good for food" (Genesis 2:9). The perfect environment for human life satisfied a dual criterion: it was both functional and artistic. The conditions for human well-being have never changed from that moment in paradise.

A similar endorsement of the nonutilitarian emerges from some of the psalms, especially the nature psalms. The Old Testament attitude toward nature was, in the words of C. S. Lewis, "a delight which is both utilitarian and poetic."[5] Psalm 104 furnishes a typical example. On the one hand, this psalm displays a farmer's attitude toward nature in which everything in the natural world is good for something. The streams, for example, "give drink to every beast of the field" (vv. 10-11). But even here the things that nature produces go beyond what is strictly needed for survival. The purpose of wine is "to gladden the heart of man," and that of oil is "to make his face shine" (v. 15) as part of a ritual of festivity. If the trees exist so "the birds of the air [may] have their habitation" in them, there is also the gratuitous fact that the birds "sing among the branches" (v. 12).

Jesus' Discourse about the Lilies

Much the same picture emerges from Jesus' famous discourse against anxiety (Matthew 6:25-34). The overall message of the discourse is that people must set a curb on the human impulse to be acquisitive and to reduce life to ceaseless striving. The specific areas to which Jesus extends his commands are food and clothing. Jesus conducts his persuasive argument by appealing to nature. He tells us to take a look around us at the birds and lilies.

As for the birds of the air, "they neither sow nor reap nor gather into barns, and yet your heavenly Father feeds them" (v. 26). The birds, in other words, are free from the utilitarian striving and anxiety that trouble human life.

Even more important for our thinking about leisure is Jesus' comment about the lilies: "Consider the lilies of the field, how they grow; they neither toil nor spin; yet I tell you, even Solomon in all his glory was not arrayed like one of these" (vv. 28-29). Here too we find a warning against the human preoccupation with the utilitarian side of life.

But more is suggested by Jesus' great aphorism commanding us to "consider the lilies of the field." Here is a call to observation and contemplation, as the antithesis to a mercenary lifestyle. Jesus' command implies a concern for the quality of our sensory and artistic life. It calls us to something as nonproductive as delighting in something beautiful.

A Christian View of Beauty

Leisure incorporates more than the enjoyment of beauty, but it certainly includes the experience of beauty. My journeys through the history of aesthetics have led me to conclude that the fate of leisure has been very much bound up with the attitude of various civilizations toward beauty. This is not surprising, since beauty is essentially something we enjoy rather than use. The beauty of a sunset or flower has no use other than to be beautiful for the glory of God and the delight of people. What, then, does the Bible say about beauty?[6]

We have already noted that God made a beautiful as well as functional world and that he planted a garden that contained "every tree that is pleasant to the sight." Psalm 19 praises the world of nature for its beauty: "The heavens are telling the glory of God; / and the firmament proclaims his handiwork" (v. 1). There is no impulse to harness nature for useful ends here. Instead we find a contemplation of nature in a spirit of worship.

The Bible even treats beauty as one of God's perfections. David "asked of the LORD . . . to behold the beauty of the LORD" (Psalm 27:4). Ezekiel describes how God bestowed his beauty upon Israel: "And your renown went forth among the nations because of your beauty, for it was perfect through the splendor which I had bestowed upon you, says the Lord GOD" (Ezekiel 16:14). Beauty belongs to God; it needs no utilitarian defense beyond that.

Elsewhere beauty merges with worship. The Old Testament worshiper could declare regarding God that "strength and beauty are in his sanctuary" (Psalm 96:6). From the King James Bible we have inherited the evocative idea of "the beauty of holiness" (for example, Psalm 29:2). The implication is that beauty, though nonutilitarian, has value in itself. The embellished priestly garments of Aaron and his sons were "for glory and for beauty" (Exodus 28:2).

What does this biblical endorsement of beauty say about leisure? It reinforces a general biblical theme of attaching value to things and activities that are not strictly useful. This overall biblical affirmation opens the way for leisure, which shares the same quality of being beyond what is utilitarian.

THE LEGITIMACY OF PLEASURE AND ENJOYMENT

The rise and fall of leisure throughout history have also been bound up with prevailing attitudes toward pleasure and enjoyment. If pleasure is regarded as bad, then obviously leisure is also bad. By definition, leisure is something we do because we want to, not because we have to.

The spirit of self-denial and asceticism (rejecting earthly pleasure as evil) has run strong in the Christian tradition. So has the sense of duty. I do not wish to deny that self-denial and duty are necessary parts of the Christian life. But they are not the whole of the Christian life. When carried beyond their legitimate place, they end up robbing the Christian life of the joy that should accompany it.

It is good to be reminded, therefore, that the Christian life is intended to be a life of God-directed enjoyment. This is the main thesis of a recent book entitled *Desiring God: Meditations of a Christian Hedonist*.[7] The author explains, "This is a serious book about being happy in God. It's about happiness because that is what our Creator commands: 'Delight yourself in the Lord' (Psalm 37:4)."

Exactly what does the Bible say about pleasure? Pleasure is one of the recurrent themes and moods in the Psalms. The writer of Psalm 16 rejoices in the fact that "the lines have fallen for me in pleasant places," (v. 6), and he asserts that at God's "right hand are pleasures for evermore" (v. 11). Equally evocative is the image we find in Psalm 36:8: God's people "feast on the abundance of thy house, / and thou givest them drink from the river of thy delights." In another Psalm we read that the "harp with the psaltery is pleasant" (Psalm 81:2, KJV).

God-centered Hedonism in the Book of Ecclesiastes

The most extended biblical affirmation of pleasure comes from the much misunderstood book of Ecclesiastes.[8] Ecclesiastes is structured on a dialectical principle of opposites. There are "under the sun" passages in which the author describes the futility of trying to find meaning and happiness in a purely earthly scale of values, and there are "above the sun" passages in which the author celebrates the God-centered life as an antidote to life "under the sun." Significantly, the affirmations of pleasure and enjoyment come from the God-centered passages. In fact, enjoyment is exactly what the writer finds denied when he limits his quest for happiness to the earthly sphere. Here are three endorsements of enjoyment that come from passages describing the God-centered life:

> There is nothing better for a man than that he should eat and drink and find enjoyment in his toil. This also, I saw, is from the hand of God; for apart from him who can eat or who can have enjoyment? For to the man who pleases him God gives wisdom and knowledge and joy (Ecclesiastes 2:24- 26).

> [God] has made everything beautiful in its time. . . . I know that there is nothing better for them than to be happy and enjoy themselves as long as they live; also that it is God's gift to man that every one should eat and drink and take pleasure in all his toil (Ecclesiastes 3:11-13).

> Behold, what I have seen to be good and to be fitting is to eat and drink and find enjoyment in all the toil with which one toils. . . . Every man also to whom God has given wealth and possessions and power to enjoy them, and to accept his lot and find enjoyment in his toil—this is the gift of God (Ecclesiastes 5:18-19).

Elsewhere the writer sounds the variations on the theme of God-given pleasure. We are commanded, for example, "Go, eat your bread with enjoyment, and drink your wine with a merry heart; for God has already approved what you do" (Ecclesiastes 9:7). Again, "Enjoy life with the wife whom you love" (Ecclesiastes 9:9). The simplest commonplaces of life are cause for pleasure to the godly person: "Light is sweet, and it is pleasant for the eyes to behold the sun" (Ecclesiastes 11:7).

Here is the ideal of godly hedonism. It is not escapist. It does not reject everyday life in favor of some other spiritual world. In fact, it is in the routine of life and work that the ancient Preacher urges us to find enjoyment. John Calvin's comment about enjoying food is very much in keeping with the spirit of the book of Ecclesiastes: "If we ponder to what end God created food," wrote Calvin, "we shall find that he meant not only to provide for necessity but also for delight and good cheer."[9]

New Testament Confirmations

This positive attitude toward enjoyment of God's good gifts continues in the New Testament. The classic passage is Paul's instruction to Timothy concerning the wealthy: "As for the rich in this world, charge them not to be haughty, nor to set their hopes on uncertain riches but on God who richly furnishes us with everything to enjoy (1 Timothy 6:17). Here we learn three important principles about enjoyment. One is that God is the giver of all good things. Second, he gives them so people can enjoy them. Third, the misuse of them consists not in the enjoyment of them but in trusting them and making idols of them.

We should also note that the biblical doctrine of heaven exalts pleasure. If heaven is the place where there is no more pain (Revelation 21:4), C. S. Lewis can correctly assert that "all pleasure is in itself a good and pain in itself an evil; if not, then the whole Christian tradition about heaven and hell and the passion of our Lord seems to have no meaning."[10]

The desire to enjoy life and seek happiness is a God implanted impulse. It can, of course, be perverted to wrong ends. It can also be killed, producing a psychological aberration that goes by the clinical name *anhedonia* ("without pleasure"). Between these extremes stands the biblical ideal: legitimate pleasure and enjoyment as God's gifts to the human race. The way to show gratitude for the gift of enjoyment is to accept it and experience it.

At stake in our view of pleasure is our view of God. Does God want people to enjoy themselves or to be miserable? The question is as simple as that. To assume that God does not want people to enjoy themselves is to charge him with being sadistic toward his creatures. As Norman Geisler writes in an article entitled "The Christian as Pleasure-Seeker," "God is not a celestial Scrooge who hates to see his children enjoy themselves."[11]

CELEBRATION AND FESTIVITY

Another biblical foundation on which we can build a case for leisure is celebration or festivity. Much leisure has the quality of celebration. Its very status as a parenthesis in the duties of life is enough to make leisure something festive. In the sense of clearing a space for us to affirm the distinctly human values, moreover, leisure leads us to celebrate human life and social relationships. Nor should we overlook the frequency with which we devote our leisure time to celebrating God's achievement in nature and human achievement in culture.

Much of our leisure is organized by society. I have in mind religious holy days such as Easter and Christmas, national holidays such as the Fourth of July and Labor Day, and seasonal celebrations such as Thanksgiving and New Year. On such days we celebrate an event or occasion. The same thing is true of such activities as the celebration of weddings, anniversaries, and birthdays.

In view of the large place such celebration and festivity play in our leisure life, we can appropriately note that they played an equally important role in the life of God's people in the Bible. Here too we can find a biblical rationale for leisure.

Religious Festivals in the Old Testament

A major piece of evidence is of course the structuring of Hebrew life around the annual calendar of holy days. Leviticus 23, for example, outlines six annual religious festivals the Israelites were instructed to keep. They are called "holy convocations" and "appointed feasts," and they were accompanied by a prohibition of labor. No doubt they resembled the American Thanksgiving Day when it is kept as a religious day.

When Moses recapitulated the Sinai laws in the form in which we find them in the book of Deuteronomy, three of the festivals were expanded to include annual pilgrimages to worship God in the temple in Jerusalem (Deuteronomy 16:16). Here we have something resembling our annual camp or retreat experiences. Group travel becomes part of the picture. So does camping out in places remote from home.

We might note in passing that the fifteen psalms that bear the common heading "A Song of Ascents" (Psalms 120-134) provide an interesting index to what went through the worshiper's mind on these occasions. These songs were sung or recited as pilgrims "went up" to Jerusalem on their annual pilgrimages. Topics for celebration in these psalms include God's providence, national security, agricultural prosperity, everyday work, family, and communal fellowship. Here, in short, is good confirmation of Josef Pieper's theory that in leisure "human values are saved and preserved."[12] The sense of exuberance and group celebration these religious pilgrimages produced is also hinted at in the glimpses we get in the worship psalms of shouting and musical performances in temple worship.

For an account of what Jewish religious festivals were really like, we can turn to the book of Nehemiah (Chapter 8). When the law was read to the remnant living in Jerusalem, "they found it written in the law that the LORD had commanded by Moses that the people of Israel should dwell in booths during the feast of the seventh month," and that they should "go out to the hills and bring branches of olive, wild olive, myrtle, palm, and other leafy trees to make booths" (vv. 14, 15). The people did just that. The result was that "there was very great rejoicing," and "they kept the feast seven days" (vv. 17, 18).

I would insist that this was a form of leisure—leisure of a specifically religious kind, but leisure nonetheless. The people camped out. They did it with other families. Social interaction ran high. Jewish tradition claims that during the feast of booths the leafy roofs should be left with cracks so the people could look up at night and see the stars in the sky. With this as a context, we might note the prayer of Ezra recorded in the next chapter of Nehemiah: "Thou art the LORD, thou alone; thou hast made heaven, the heaven of heavens, with all their host . . . and the host of heaven worships thee" (Nehemiah 9:6).

For yet another glimpse at the Old Testament practice of celebration and festivity, we can look at the festival of Purim. The origin of the festival was the deliverance of the Jews from the plot of Haman through the heroism of Esther. On the day after the Jews had defended themselves against their enemies, "they rested and made that a day of feasting and gladness" (Esther 9:17). In later Jewish history, it became "a day for gladness and feasting and holiday-making, and a day on which they send choice portions to one another" (Esther 9:19).

Private Feasting and Hospitality

In addition to the officially prescribed holy days of biblical times, we read about private feasting and hospitality. These too were forms of leisure—pleasurable social activities conducted with an air of festivity.

The "classic" among these stories is of course the meal Abraham and Sarah prepared for three angelic visitors (Genesis 18:1-8). The event meets all the criteria of a leisure occasion. It is set apart from ordinary daily life. The three visitors rest under a tree while Abraham and Sarah, as ideal hosts, prepare a meal. A lavish meal it is, replete with cakes, curds, milk, and roast beef. Having provided the materials for leisure, Abraham stands by under a tree while his guests eat and then enters into conversation with them after the meal. The New Testament commentary on this event confirms what I have said about it: "Do not neglect to show hospitality to strangers, for thereby some have entertained angels unawares" (Hebrews 13:2). It was, indeed, an occasion of festive entertainment and leisure.

Eating and Drinking with Jesus

The pattern of religious and social leisure we have noted in the Old Testament carries over to the New Testament, where the chief example is Jesus. The wedding party Jesus attended at Cana in Galilee (John 2:1-11) was simultaneously a social and religious occasion. It was a wedding celebration carried out according to the best ceremonial rules, as evidenced by the large water jars for purification rituals that figure prominently in the story. Not only did the presence of Jesus at such a party lend sanction to it—he actually turned water into wine to keep the party going. C. S. Lewis interprets the event thus: "The miracle at Cana in Galilee by sanctifying an innocent, sensuous pleasure could be taken to sanctify . . . a recreational use of culture—mere 'entertainment.'"[13]

We see here in microcosm something that pervades the Gospels. If we arranged Jesus' life during his public years into a few composite portraits, one of these would be a picture of Jesus attending a dinner or party. It could be rightly said of him that "the Son of man has come eating and drinking" (Luke 7:34). Jesus' critics were offended at such behavior, saying, "Behold, a glutton and a drunkard, a friend of tax collectors and sinners!" (7:34).

What the Biblical Endorsement of Celebration Means to Leisure

I have sampled what the Bible implicitly says about celebration and festivity by looking selectively at three sets of data—the religious festivals of God's people, entertainment of guests, and the convivial lifestyle of Jesus. Together these tell us something important about the legitimacy of leisure. Two writers on the theology of leisure have elaborated this very point.

Josef Pieper makes celebration and the feast the center of leisure.[14] He writes that "the soul of leisure . . . lies in 'celebration.'" The meaning of celebration, moreover, "is man's affirmation of the universe and his experiencing the world in an aspect other than its everyday one." And because he writes as a Christian, Pieper believes that the basis of true celebration is divine worship. There can be no festival or marriage without God, writes Pieper, and nothing shows this more clearly than the emptiness that accompanies celebrations devoid of a sense of worship. He speaks of the difference between "a living and deeply traditional feast day, with its roots in divine worship, and one of those rootless celebrations, carefully and unspontaneously prepared beforehand, and as artificial as a maypole."

Harvey Cox has written at much greater length about the intersections between leisure and festivity.[15] Festivity, he writes, is a form of play, "the special time when ordinary chores are set aside while man celebrates some event, affirms the sheer goodness of what is, or observes the memory of a god or hero." It is a distinctly human activity. In Cox's view, "Man is *homo festivus*," but forces in modern culture have conspired to the point where "man's celebrative . . . faculties have atrophied." Christianity has failed to preserve the elements of festive leisure it once supplied to Western culture.

PLAY IN THE BIBLE

The dimensions of leisure we have covered thus far have tended toward the aesthetic and social forms. In Jesus' command to consider the lilies of the field, for example, we have a call to contemplation and enjoyment of artistic beauty. In his attendance at dinner parties we see leisure as conversation and social interaction. We can balance that picture by seeing what the Bible says about play and sport. The evidence will not be plentiful, but it deserves attention.

One of the passages occurs in the book of Proverbs (8:30-31). As a way of praising the divine origin of wisdom, the writer develops a creation story in which Wisdom, personified as a woman, pictures herself as being present when God created the world. Some translators believe that Wisdom is portrayed as "a child without a care . . . the vivacious playmate of God and man, with heaven and earth as her playground."[16] A translation from the Jewish Publication Society clearly reflects this understanding:

> Then I [Wisdom] was by Him, as a nursling;
> And I was daily all delight,
> Playing always before Him,
> Playing in His habitable earth,
> And my delights are with the sons of men.[17]

The Jerusalem Bible translation is similar:

> I was by his side, a master craftsman,
>   delighting him day after day,
>   ever at play in his presence,
> at play everywhere in his world,
>   delighting to be with the sons of men.

The general meaning of the passage is clear: it is a mark of wisdom to delight and play in God's world.

A parallel passage can be found in Psalm 104, a psalm that catalogs the provisions God has created nature to supply. One of these is play or sport. God is said to have created Leviathan "to sport [frolic, NIV]" in the sea (v. 26). Here too we find a brief affirmation of an important aspect of leisure—the impulse to abandon oneself in play in the world God has made for the provision of his creatures. In the description of Behemoth (possibly the hippopotamus or the elephant) in the book of Job, we see a picture of the mountains "where all the wild beasts play" (40:20).

The Playfulness of Jesus

To the Old Testament data we can add the example of Jesus. I refer not to his actions but to his words. There is a playfulness and humor in the sayings of Jesus that at least touch upon the current topic.

This has been documented at fullest length in Elton Trueblood's small classic *The Humor of Christ*.[18] Trueblood sets out "to challenge the conventionalized picture of a Christ who never laughed . . . by reference to deeds as well as to words." Rejecting the "assumption that Christ never joked," Trueblood shows that the sayings and parables of Jesus show continuous humor. The most characteristic form of that humor was the giantesque—the hilarious exaggeration, the preposterous fantasy, the "Texas story, which no one believes literally, but which everyone remembers." Trueblood's final conclusion relates to the argument of this book: "If Christ laughed a great deal, as the evidence shows, and if He is what He claimed to be, we cannot avoid the logical conclusion that there is laughter and gaiety in the heart of God."

There is present in the humor of Christ the same *spirit* that underlies much leisure. That spirit is characterized by such qualities as nonseriousness, a letting go of formality and inhibition, high-spiritedness, and spontaneity. We might even speak of the fun impulse evident in Jesus' humor, and we know that a main purpose of leisure is simply to have fun. The light-heartedness of Jesus is all the more noteworthy because he was also the man of sorrows, acquainted with grief.

Play in the Coming Kingdom

Another strand in the biblical attitude toward play emerges from the eschatological pictures of the coming kingdom. Not only is there the rest that remains for the people of God (Hebrews 4:9-10), there is also the play that will characterize the future kingdom. Here are three specimen descriptions:

> And the streets of the city shall be full of boys and girls playing in its streets (Zechariah 8:5).

> The city shall be rebuilt upon its mound,
> and the palace shall stand where it used to be.
> Out of them shall come songs of thanksgiving,
> and the voices of those who make merry.
> (Jeremiah 30:18-19)

Again you shall adorn yourself with timbrels,
and shall go forth in the dance of the merrymakers.

. . . .

Then shall the maidens rejoice in the dance,
and the young men and the old shall be merry.
I will turn their mourning into joy,
I will comfort them, and give them gladness for
sorrow.
I will feast the soul of the priests with abundance,
and my people shall be satisfied with my goodness.
(Jeremiah 31:4, 13-14)

If this type of playful celebration will characterize the perfect society, it should be a part of the redeemed life now as well.

THE EFFECTS OF SIN

Thus far I have painted a positive picture of what the Bible says about leisure. But we know that leisure did not escape the effects of the Fall. Human sinfulness is at least as evident in the world of human leisure as it is in the world of work. We get a few pictures of this in the Bible, but of course more abundant evidence emerges when we simply look around at what people are doing in their leisure time.

In human history, leisure has always had the potential to degenerate into immorality. A brief list of such leisure pursuits appears in Galatians 5, where Paul mentions some of the things that make up "the works of the flesh," including immortality, impurity, licentiousness, drunkenness, carousing, "and the like" (5:19-21).

There is something inherently self-indulgent about leisure in that it is something with which we reward ourselves. This is not necessarily bad, but it can always cross the line into self-centered indulgence. For the rich farmer in Jesus' parable, this is exactly what happened. Having earned the means for leisure, the farmer became self-indulgent in his hedonism, as captured by his inner dialogue: "Soul, you have ample goods laid up for many years; take your ease, eat, drink, be merry" (Luke 12:19). God pronounces this leisure enthusiast a fool for his complacent and worldly minded hedonism.

Another picture of self-defeating hedonism emerges from the book of Ecclesiastes. I have already noted that book's affirmation of pleasure when it is accepted as a gift from God. But the writer also pictures a frantic quest that he undertook to find meaning in pleasure "under the sun." The result of this purely humanistic experiment in living was a dead end:

> I said to myself, "Come now, I will make a test of pleasure; enjoy yourself." But behold, this also was vanity. I said of laughter, "It is mad," and of pleasure, "What use is it?" (Ecclesiastes 2:1-2).

The writer proceeds to outline his hedonistic quest, proving his claim that "I kept my heart from no pleasure" (v. 10). But this hedonist, like many in our own culture, came up empty: "Behold, all was vanity and as striving after wind, and there was nothing to be gained under the sun" (v. 11).

Perhaps the perversions of leisure we have noted seem like the gross forms. But the abuse of leisure can also happen to the highly cultured and refined. Cultural activities have the same potential to degenerate that life in the local bar does. The prophet Amos makes music the symbol of a society that has lapsed into triviality, and he puts it into a context of selfish indulgence that is always one of the dangers of leisure. He pictures people who "stretch themselves upon their couches," who "sing idle songs to the sound of the harp," who "drink wine in bowls," and who "anoint themselves with the finest oils" (Amos 6:4-6). His warning is that "the revelry of those who stretch themselves shall pass away" (v. 7). The picture is as up-to-date as what we glimpse in the latest American magazines.

The perversions of leisure in our time have expanded the list of abuses. Boredom continues to be a problem for many, especially the retired. The search for distraction seems to afflict the young, at video arcades and elsewhere. Many people are lonely in their leisure time, while others long for time away from the crowd. There are mindless and mind-numbing leisure pursuits. And there are excursions into illicit sex, pornography, and drugs. What this list tells us is that leisure is not exempt from moral judgment, though a secular culture tends to treat it as exempt. Faced with the enormity of moral problems posed by leisure pursuits in a secular society, the church has tended to act as though leisure itself is ignoble and not something with which Christians should dirty their hands. This has had tragic consequences. The voice of conscience has frequently been lost in society's leisure, and Christians themselves, pretending they are above leisure, have actually gravitated to a low level of leisure pursuits by default.

LEISURE AND THE REDEEMED LIFE

At the heart of the Christian faith is the experience of redemption, the return to a state that was lost. Psalm 23 describes how the shepherd (metaphorically God) restores the vitality of a sheep's life by leading it to noontime rest in a lush, shady oasis. Leisure is such an oasis in the world of work and duty.

Leisure shares the redemptive principle with Christianity. It aims to bring a person back to physical, mental, and emotional strength and wholeness. We can perhaps regain the fullness of meaning in a word that has become somewhat trivialized in current usage by inserting an unexpected hyphen in *re-creation*. The purpose of leisure is to re-create a person—to restore him or her to an earlier condition.

Ralph Glasser, writing from the perspective of the social sciences, believes that in leisure people pursue an ideal identity they have created for themselves.[19] But as Glasser notes, in a secular society that has lost its spiritual roots, the ideal identity of people is confused and emaciated. In the words of one sociologist of leisure, "Separated from [a] spiritual view, the idea of recreation has the aimless circularity of simply restoring us to a state in which we can best continue our work."[20]

The Christian faith supplies depth to the very idea of leisure. The person in Christ has an identity toward which to aspire. Leisure, because it is "the growing time of the human spirit" and a time "for rest and restoration, for rediscovering life in its entirety,"[21] provides space for a Christian to re-establish that identity.

Within this context, I trust that my claim for the kinship between worship and leisure is convincing. Both worship and leisure require that we call a temporary halt to our work and active duties. Both equip us for life by temporarily removing us from life. They also share the goal of re-creation and refreshment and recalling us to our true selves. Worship and prayer raise leisure to a spiritual plane, but in function they share the place of leisure in our lives. That is why Josef Pieper, who has a high view of leisure as "a condition of the soul," believes that the basis of leisure is divine worship. "Cut off from the worship of the divine," Pieper writes, "leisure becomes laziness and work inhuman."[22]

In an earlier chapter we noted that the Christian sense of duty to God and humanity has a tendency to rob Christians of much of their leisure time. But there is also an asset in the Christian life. Many of the spiritual exercises of worship fulfill the needs of leisure. While non-Christians snore on Sunday morning, Christians are allowing the worship of God to re-create them.

SUMMARY: A THEOLOGY OF LEISURE

I trust that the foregoing discussion shows how inaccurate it is to say, "we must not expect to derive from the Bible any explicit guidance upon the right use of leisure."[23] The Bible provides both a general rationale for leisure and guidelines for how to pursue leisure.

A theology of leisure begins with the biblical doctrine of creation. When God created the world, he himself rested from work. Divine rest, in turn, became the model for God's command that people, too, must punctuate their work with times of rest and worship. The doctrine of creation also shows us that human life is not intended to consist only of what is useful, just as God's creation is more than functional.

The Bible also tells us about the quality of life God intends for people. Pleasure is good in principle. Celebration of life and festivity are ingredients of the good life. So are play and fun.

The fall of the human race into sin of course affected leisure. It made possible the abuse of leisure in such forms as immorality and self-centered indulgence. But leisure, like other things in life, can be redeemed from abuse. In fact, leisure itself is a form of redemption or re-creation. As such, it can become part of our life of worship as we renew our identity in Christ as citizens of his world and kingdom.

FURTHER READING

Josef Pieper, *Leisure the Basis of Culture* (1952).

Harold D. Lehman, *In Praise of Leisure* (1974).

Lewis B. Smedes, "Theology and the Playful Life," pp. 46-62 in *God and the Good*, ed. Clifton Orlebeke and Lewis Smedes (1975).

Robert K. Johnston, *The Christian at Play* (1983).

Leland Ryken, *Culture in Christian Perspective* (1986).

Chapter 7, Notes

1. A. Alt, as quoted in Robert K. Johnston, *The Christian at Play* (Grand Rapids, Mich.: Wm. B. Eerdmans Publishing Co., 1983), 88-89. Johnston notes others who agree with this view of the prehistory of the sabbath.

2. Josef Pieper, *Leisure the Basis of Culture*, trans. Alexander Dru (New York: Pantheon Books, 1952, 1964), 28.

3. Lee W. Gibbs, as quoted in Johnston, 43.

4. Virginia Stem Owens, "On Praising God with Our Senses," in *The Christian Imagination: Essays on Literature and the Arts*, ed. Leland Ryken (Grand Rapids, Mich.: Baker Book House, 1981), 379.

5. C. S. Lewis, *Reflections on the Psalms* (New York: Harcourt, Brace and World, 1958), 77.

6. For more on the subject than I say here, see my book *Culture in Christian Perspective: A Door to Understanding and Enjoying the Arts* (Portland, Ore.: Multnomah Press, 1986), 70ff.

7. John Piper, *Desiring God: Meditations of a Christian Hedonist* (Portland, Ore.: Multnomah Press, 1986).

8. For a more extended discussion of the book of Ecclesiastes along the lines I suggest here, see my book *Words of Delight: A Literary Introduction to the Bible* (Grand Rapids, Mich.: Baker Book House, 1987).

9. John Calvin, *Institutes of the Christian Religion* , ed. John T. McNeill (Philadelphia: Westminster Press, 1960), 1:720.

10. C. S. Lewis, *Christian Reflections* (Grand Rapids, Mich.: Wm. B. Eerdmans Publishing Co., 1967), 21.

11. Norman Geisler, "The Christian as Pleasure-Seeker," *Christianity Today*, 25 September 1975, 11.

12. Pieper, 2.

13. Lewis, *Christian Reflections*, 15.

14. Pieper, 44-46.

15. Harvey Cox, *The Feast of Fools: A Theological Essay on Festivity and Fantasy* (New York: Harper and Row, 1969).

16. William McKane, *Proverbs: A New Approach* (Philadelphia: Westminster Press, 1970), 357.

17. Proverbs 8:30-31, translation of the Jewish Publication Society of America, as found in W. Gunther Plaut, *Book of Proverbs: A Commentary* (New York: Union of American Hebrew Congregations, 1961), 113-14.

18. Elton Trueblood, *The Humor of Christ* (New York: Harper and Row, 1964).

19. Ralph Glasser, "Leisure Policy, Identity and Work," in *Work and Leisure*, ed. J. T. Haworth and M. A. Smith (Princeton: Princeton Book Company, 1976), 36-52.

20. Stanley Parker, *The Sociology of Leisure* (New York: International Publications Service, 1976), p. 107.

21. Robert Lee, *Religion and Leisure in America* (Nashville: Abingdon Press, 1964), 35.

22. Pieper, 48.

23. Alan Richardson, *The Biblical Doctrine of Work* (London: SCM, 1952), 51.

Chapter 8

The Ethics of Leisure

A theology of leisure informs our thinking about leisure. The ethics of leisure is concerned with what we plan to do on the basis of that theology. Much of what I say in this chapter can be placed under the umbrella of stewardship—serving God responsibly with what he has given us.

LEISURE AS THE ARENA OF MORAL CHOICE

The ethics of leisure begins with an awareness that leisure presents us with unavoidable choices. The first choice is whether to accept the responsibility to make time for leisure. Once we have made time for leisure, further choices confront us—many more choices than we usually face in regard to work.

Frank Gaebelein, in an essay entitled "The Christian Use of Leisure," wrote that "the very word *leisure* implies responsibility. . . . We are accountable for the stewardship of our leisure as well as of our working time."[1] Harold Lehman writes in similar terms:

> Leisure time is the arena of choice. Here we must make decisions every day about how to use free

207

time. We cannot evade leisure-time choices, even a non-choice amounts to a choice by default.[2]

Choice by default is exactly what often prevails. The leisure patterns of most Christians are much the same as those of a secular culture. We have not been encouraged to become self-conscious about our leisure choices, nor have we given adequate attention to educating ourselves to upgrade the quality of our leisure.

If God calls us to be good stewards of our leisure time, the choices we make are necessarily moral choices. C. S. Lewis has noted this particularly well:

> Our leisure, even our play, is a matter of serious concern. There is no neutral ground in the universe; every square inch, every split second, is claimed by God and counterclaimed by Satan. . . . It is a serious matter to choose wholesome recreations.[3]

If we realized the urgency of the matter, we would not so aimlessly plop down in front of the television to watch whatever happens to be on. To be truly moral about our leisure will require us to attach the value to it that it deserves.

ALLOWING LEISURE TO BE LEISURE

It is a principle of ethics that something should be allowed to have the integrity of what it truly is. God created the world purposefully. Creatures in God's world have a *telos*—a created end for which they were created and toward which they tend.

The commonest form of violating this principle in regard to leisure is to turn leisure, which is inherently nonutilitarian, into something utilitarian. Leisure should carry its own reward and be fulfilling in itself. But the human race has found ways to twist that purpose.

One way to do so is to treat leisure as an appendage to work. In such a climate, people value leisure only as it contributes to their ability to work. The results are detrimental to leisure. People who are preoccupied with work in this way give little time to leisure. The quality of the little leisure these people have is often low. People who have studied workaholics find that their leisure often degenerates into idleness or passivity and sometimes consists wholly of sleeping.

Other people fall into the trap of working at their play. They try to get work time results from something intended to be nonwork. They read for improvement, so that reading becomes *homework*. Physical exercise becomes *working out*. By the time leisure has been filtered through the work mentality, it has frequently ceased to be leisure and is instead a form of work.

Another feature of leisure that can easily get violated is its status as a break from the obligations of life. It is, in the best sense of the word, an escape. Pleasurable work does not meet this test. People who enjoy their work and therefore work pretty much all the time have not found a place for leisure in their lives, although they have achieved an ideal of leisure-in-work.

In order for leisure to be an escape, we must also leave behind the competitive spirit that often characterizes the workplace. Relaxation is one of the inherent qualities of leisure. Compulsively competitive people often fail to draw a boundary around the competitive impulse and thereby twist leisure from its intended purpose. When they play games, they drive themselves to win and spoil the occasion for everyone with their unhappiness when they lose.

I must also return to the point made in the previous chapter about the goodness of pleasure and enjoyment. Leisure is rooted in an ethic of responsible pleasure. To live morally in the realm of leisure is to cultivate the ability to enjoy life outside of work.

We should also note how quickly the act of using something (the utilitarian ethic) destroys our ability to enjoy it. In subdividing a field, we lose the beauty of the landscape. In building a house, we lose what was pleasing about the trees used for lumber. When we eat an apple, we forfeit our ability to enjoy its attractiveness.

There is something analogous to these physical examples in the realm of leisure (with the exception of leisure pursuits that involve making something and in which the product is part of the pleasure). Leisure activities should be self-rewarding. In the sense of not using them but simply enjoying them, we should (paradoxical as it may sound) come away from them empty-handed, "with nothing left to us but a memory of delight, an increase in well-being so deep and so central and so invisibly distributed throughout the psyche that it cannot even be located."[4] Gordon Dahl has noted that "the work ethic has inspired a morality of use; the leisure ethic will inspire a morality of enjoyment."[5]

LEISURE AS A PERSONAL RESPONSIBILITY

An important part of the morality of leisure is the relationship of leisure to the individual. In fact, we will speak of that relationship as an obligation.

In the previous chapter we talked about leisure as a creation ordinance. God created people with the capacity and need for rest and pleasure. He gave commands that obligate people to set a boundary to their work and other responsibilities of life. On one occasion Jesus protected his busy disciples from themselves by sending them away from the crowd (Mark 6:30-31).

It would appear, therefore, that the title of Wayne Oates book *Your Right to Rest* understates the moral obligation we all face in regard to leisure.[6] Rest is not only something to which we have a right, but also something to which we have an obligation.

Leisure is something we owe to ourselves. For one thing, our mental, physical, and emotional well-being require it. One of the common problems in the work force today is burnout, which in its lesser form is simply fatigue and stress. One study of employees in eighteen organizations found that nearly half of the workers suffered from psychological burnout.[7] Burnout and unrelieved stress are not God's goal for human life. Leisure is one of the protections God has given to the human race against ceaseless work, whether physical, mental, or religious.

Living morally in God's world includes living in accordance with the kind of creatures God made us to be. Not only the Bible but the human social sciences as well tell us that we are leisure-seeking creatures. Human nature craves more than work and more than utilitarianism. To indulge this capacity is not selfish. In fact, it can have within it an element of unselfishness, of letting go of one's urge to acquire and be successful, of relinquishing one's status that in our culture is so closely bound up in one's work. I do not deny that leisure can assume the quality of selfish indulgence, but it just as often has the opposite quality of allowing people to get beyond themselves.

Wayne Oates speaks of the self-deception of trying to live as if we do not have a body.[8] When people deceive themselves in this way, they operate on the premise that their spiritual energy and service to God have nothing to do with their bodies. This, too, is a self-defeating way of life. It also happens to be a heresy, since the Bible is very clear that God made us physical creatures and that our bodies are important. The doctrines of creation and the resurrection of the body leave no doubt about the matter.

The Bible also speaks clearly about the importance of serving God in our physical activities. A classic text is 1 Corinthians 10:31, which states, "So, whether you eat or drink, or whatever you do, do all to the glory of God." Romans 12:1 is equally important: "I appeal to you therefore . . . to present your bodies as a living sacrifice, holy and acceptable to God, which is your spiritual worship." Because we are physical creatures subject to physical and psychological laws, to have regular times of leisure is to live in accord with the Creator's plan for us.

Another feature of our make-up that leisure helps to fulfill is our need for rewards. We do not have to accept untenable theories of behavioralism in order to agree with modern psychology that people function best when they receive rewards for their effort. The Bible takes a similar approach. It is filled with talk about the rewards of the righteous and the diligent. Ecclesiastes 4:9 speaks of those who "have a good reward for their toil." Or consider the well-known comment by Paul that "the labourer is worthy of his reward" (1 Timothy 5:18, KJV).

Leisure can be regarded as one of the rewards that come from labor. It is something God wants the worker to have. A work ethic based solely on the premise that we work in order to make leisure possible is of course deficient, since it robs work of its character as a calling from God. But in a more modest sense I do not see why we would find it objectionable that we work partly to make leisure possible. To work in order to have time to fulfill and develop ourselves and enrich our relationships in leisure pursuits is a more worthy motivation for work than the urge to acquire more and more things.

Jesus' comment that "a man's life does not consist in the abundance of his possessions" (Luke 12:15) is a foundational principle in a Christian leisure ethic. It asserts that a rich life requires more than ceaseless acquisition. Leisure is one of these nonacquisitive ingredients of the good life.

We might also listen to the wisdom of the utopian tradition. Writers of utopias tend to have naively unrealistic attitudes toward work. They act as if the drudgery of work does not even exist. But on the subject of leisure this same utopian tradition contains accurate insights into the deep-seated human longing for fulfilling leisure.

As was noted in chapter 3, Thomas More, who wrote the first self-conscious utopia, describes a country where people work only six hours a day. More's utopians do not dislike work; they have simplified their lifestyle in order "to give all citizens as much time as public needs permit for freeing and developing their minds." They rest two hours after dinner. They read and attend public lectures. They love gardening. After supper they "spend an hour in some recreation, in summer gardening, in winter diverting themselves in their dining halls with music or talk."

There is, of course, an element of wishful thinking in any utopia. But that is exactly the point. The utopian tradition clarifies human values and envisions a better world than the one we inhabit. When writers of utopias treat enlightened leisure as a major reward of work, they are telling us something we need to know.

In addition to making us physical creatures who need rest and reward, God made us time-bound creatures. To take time for leisure pursuits is to submit to our status as time-bound people. Robert Lee is right to stress time as an important element in a Christian leisure ethic.[9] The most common way to deny the limitations of time is to work frantically in an effort to get everything done. In ceaseless work we harbor the illusion that we are not under time after all.

Furthermore, our own society lives by the rule that time is money. Within such a context, to find time for leisure is to stop striving against the limitations of time. It is an acknowledgment that we cannot do everything and that at a certain point we need to let go of the acquisitive impulse.

To accept the responsibility of leisure is to show a concern for the quality of our experiences in time, not simply their quantity. An overly stimulated lifestyle is as much a foe to leisure as is idleness. The goal of leisure is not to multiply distractions but to make our life abundant. Lee summarizes the importance of time to the concept of leisure:

> A Christian understanding of time beckons us to accept all time as God's gift, including our leisure; to live our leisure in terms of the quality of its events; to be willing to commit ourselves to act during leisure; and to open ourselves to the joy of living leisure in the creative love of God and man.[10]

A final dimension of leisure in its relation to oneself is that leisure provides opportunities to discover and develop ourselves as individuals. Freed from obligations, we are free to be ourselves. There is a sense in which leisure provides the time for us to get in touch with ourselves. Introspection is a necessary ingredient (though not the only ingredient) of a full leisure life.

So is solitude. We have perhaps heard too much in recent years about the social dimension of leisure. We have even been made to feel guilty about time spent by ourselves. To spend leisure time by oneself, we are told, is narcissistic and antisocial.

I cannot agree. One of the great deficiencies in our fast-paced society is that many people have lost the values that come from spending time alone. The French philosopher Blaise Pascal found already in his day that "all the unhappiness of men arises from one single fact, that they cannot stay quietly in their own chamber."[11] When we do not find time for solitude in our leisure we cut ourselves off from one of the richest sources of personal discovery and renewal. We learn things about ourselves and develop ourselves in solitude in ways that we do not when we are with others.

THE SOCIAL FUNCTION OF LEISURE

Leisure provides the opportunity for relating to oneself, but its function does not stop there. Leisure is inherently (though not exclusively) social. Many leisure activities occur in group settings. Leisure is considered a responsibility of society and government, all the way from buying park land and building recreational facilities to running city recreational programs and sponsoring cultural events.

The social dimension of leisure is itself enough to make it a concern for Christians. The Bible portrays people as finding full meaning only in relationship to other people and God. We are intended to live with other people. Given this Christian view of the person as a relational being, leisure becomes a key ingredient in the Christian life. Freed from the obligations of daily living, in leisure we can enjoy people and activities for their own sake.

Leisure and the Family

The family is perhaps the most important social arena within which leisure occurs. We have not been accustomed to regard leisure as a responsibility of the Christian family, but we should begin to look upon it in this light. Families have the potential to spend more time together in leisure activities than in working together. But it is only a potential.

The first step toward accepting the moral responsibility to cultivate family relationships in leisure is to curb the tendency for family members to disperse from each other and join people of their own age group. We live in a highly specialized society, and our leisure patterns tend to reflect this. In giving in to this cultural pattern, Christian families have lost many opportunities to build family unity through shared leisure experiences, and this at a time when the family is losing its force as an institution in our society.

The responsibility of a Christian family in regard to leisure extends beyond simply doing leisure activities together. Education for leisure is also a family responsibility, especially for the parents. I say this because leisure always reflects the values of people, and Christian parents are responsible to instill the best possible values in their children.

In general, children learn their leisure patterns from the home. If there are no clear directions available in the home, they will naturally learn their leisure patterns elsewhere. I cannot overemphasize that leisure is a learned behavior and that people do in their leisure time what they have learned to do. To ignore the importance of inculcating leisure values in children is a great abdication of parental duty.

We need to say one more thing about the moral duty of leisure with regard to one's family. Earlier we said that leisure is something an individual owes to himself or herself. People whose vocation is also their avocation—who continue to do off the job what they do on the job because this is what they most enjoy doing—might seem to constitute a partial exception. After all, the foremost scholar of workaholics found that they tend to be happy with their lifestyle.

But when placed into a moral framework of responsibility to family, another conclusion emerges: People have an obligation to their families to participate in leisure activities together.

Leisure and Friendships

The family is one of the social arenas within which leisure occurs. Friendships are a second. Without shared leisure pursuits, many of our friendships would be anemic and would eventually die. Most friendships require leisure as a nurturing agent.

Many things make up the leisure that is available to friends. One is conversation and the sharing of meals. The Bible portrays hospitality as a moral virtue. We often think of hospitality as a duty or obligation (and often it is), but the festivity of extending or receiving hospitality is just as much a part of this virtue.

Participating in leisure activities together is another dimension of leisure in friendship. Of course it takes additional planning to go to an event with another family or with other people, but the payoffs are high. I think of occasions when my wife and I attended concerts, films, and picnics with another couple as leisure time well spent.

In talking about the role of leisure in family living and friendships, I am impressed again by the way in which leisure clears a space for the recovery of distinctly human values. To nurture family bonds and friendships is surely a Christian virtue.

Leisure and the Church

Leisure reaches beyond the family and our circle of friends to include the church as well. Several things make up the responsibility of the church in regard to leisure.

One is to assert a Christian view of leisure from the pulpit and in the classroom. Many churchgoers would be surprised to be told that one can think Christianly about leisure. For one thing, we should not take for granted that the person in the pew believes leisure is good. Commitment to work, to achievement, and to Christian service runs strong in most Protestant churches.

Of course the opposite situation also exists. Some church people are so busy pursuing leisure activities that they are seldom or never available for service within the church. Television and sports have made the Sunday evening service obsolete in many churches. In such cases the church needs to preach a message of moderation in leisure and balance in the Christian life.

In general, the church in our century has ignored the issue of leisure. It would be easy to get the impression that Christians should be above indulging in leisure. The truth is, of course, that no one in our culture gets by without spending some time in leisure activities. By pretending that they are exempt from leisure, many Christians drift by default into a relatively low quality leisure life.

In addition to providing direction to people's thinking about leisure, the church has an obligation to provide occasions for leisure among its members. The churches I have known deserve high marks for providing leisure activities for their members, though this is somewhat concealed by the fact that these activities usually go by the name of social events rather than leisure. Even attending a worship service often includes the leisure dimension of greeting friends.

I have come away from the writing of this book with a new appreciation for the legitimacy of church-sponsored leisure activities. Youth programs require them, but so do adult programs. If sociologists are right about the function of leisure in relating people to each other and to groups, I do not see how we can escape the conclusion that much of what the New Testament epistles say about the unity of believers can be fostered and expressed by shared leisure activities, all the way from visiting in each other's homes to attending events together.

We should not make too sharp a distinction between the spiritual and social aspects of the church. The church is first of all a spiritual fellowship, to be sure. But with that as a base, it is also an institution made up of people with normal human needs. These needs include sociability, relaxation, and enjoyment. In our efforts to avoid the liberals' error of turning the church into a social club, we must not ignore the need for human fellowship and shared enjoyment.

I return also to my earlier point that spiritual exercises such as worship services, Bible studies, and prayer groups share some of the same qualities as leisure. They remove us from the world of work and daily obligation and then send us back to that world refreshed. They clear a space for important values to reassert themselves. If I am right in these observations, church life contains within it at least a partial counterbalance to its tendency also, with its duties and activities, to rob people of leisure time.

We should say something too about the relationship between Sunday observance and leisure. As we noted in the previous chapter, the sabbath rest that can be traced all the way back to God's rest after the work of creation provides a rationale for leisure. But what we do on Sunday is also a practical moral issue, in that sabbath observance is part of the moral law known as the Ten Commandments. The fourth commandment prescribes the sabbath as a holy day, not the holiday our secular culture has made it. When I say that I have become convinced that leisure has important connections to Sunday observance, I am not recommending desecration of the Lord's Day.

Yet Sunday must feel leisurely and relaxed in order to rank as a day of rest from work. For many conscientious workers in the church, Sunday is not a day of rest. It is a day of physical and emotional exertion that leaves them drained. We need to respect the principle of leisure in Sunday observance, especially leisure in the sense of feeling free from the obligations of life.

The church needs to acknowledge the problem before solutions are likely to be effective. In some cases the church program may have to be scaled down in order to free people from what is, after all, work on Sunday. And in the home, perhaps the conventional elaborate Sunday dinner, for all its positive virtues, needs to be simplified. Or perhaps some of the work related to a lavish dinner can be done on Saturday.

LEISURE AS STEWARDSHIP TO GOD

Leisure relates us to God as well as to ourselves and other people. For one thing, leisure is God's gift to us. Rest from labor was a creation ordinance and part of God's provision for the human race. When God created the perfect environment and lifestyle, he included not only food to sustain life but also "every tree that is pleasant to the sight" (Genesis 2:9).

If God is the source of leisure, the proper response is obviously gratitude to the Giver. It is no wonder that we find it natural to thank God for our enjoyable leisure experiences. The enjoyment is incomplete until it is expressed in gratitude to God. We are often most conscious of God during leisure occasions, all the way from an encounter with the beauty of nature to celebration of a birthday to observance of a holiday to the enjoyment of fine music. Any activity with this potential for joining people to their God deserves to be protected and nurtured.

Perhaps the presence or absence of a Godward orientation is a touchstone by which we can measure the relative worthiness of leisure pursuits. In any case, to view leisure as a form of stewardship influences the types of leisure activities a person chooses.

On the one hand, it rules out leisure activities that are immoral. A lot of leisure activities involve violence, for example. A number of sports, such as boxing and wrestling, fit that description. Violence is a staple in many movies and television dramas. To open oneself up to the spectacle of violence cannot possibly be good stewardship of leisure time.

Other types of immorality are plentiful on the contemporary leisure scene as well. Pornography, all the way from the subtle to the blatant, has infiltrated the world of reading, viewing, and music. In more general terms, leisure activities always presuppose certain values. What we do in our leisure time supports some values and undermines others. What goes on at a typical rock concert undermines Christian moral values. So do many movies and television programs. As stewards of our leisure time, we have a moral obligation to reject leisure activities that are hostile to Christian values.

On the positive side, regarding leisure as stewardship to God encourages good leisure pursuits. A profitable way to analyze this is to consider the types of stewardship we exercise in our leisure.

Types of Stewardship in Leisure

In leisure we exercise stewardship of time. Time has value because it is the gift of God and the arena within which we live out our lives before God. The most succinct statement of the biblical view of time is the third chapter of Ecclesiastes, where we view time from both a human and divine perspective. From a human perspective, there is "a time for every matter under heaven" (vv. 1-8), including both work and leisure. God, for his part, "has made everything beautiful in its time" (v. 11). God also uses time to test people (v. 18) and to judge them, "for he has appointed a time for every matter, and for every work" (v. 17). Time is the medium of our existence. God takes it seriously, and so should we.

To be a good steward of time means to use it well, with gratitude to God who gave it. This applies equally to our work and our play. To use time well begins with a concern not simply for the quantity of time we have at our disposal but the quality of it. The content we give to our time, including our leisure time, is what counts. Good leisure is thus more than mere distraction. It is the infusion of positive experiences into one's life.

Another way of saying this is that we are called to *be* as well as to *do*. Our attitude toward time determines our attitude toward leisure. "Time is money," says the utilitarian ethic. But such a narrow view of the possibilities of time fails to do justice to the kind of people God made us to be.

When we defined leisure in the opening chapter, we noted that it is more than free time and more than certain activities that the human race has decided to categorize as leisure pursuits. Leisure is also a quality of life and a state of being. The same can be said of time, which is not a mere quantity but something for whose quality we are responsible. The right question to ask is, "In this moment, in this activity, in this relationship, am I all that I can be or ought to be?" The way we answer that question will influence how we spend our leisure time.

In addition to exercising stewardship of time in our leisure, we are called to exercise stewardship of God's world. The creation mandate in which God commanded the human race to "have dominion over" the world (Genesis 1:26, 28) is usually interpreted as a summons to work. But this is an arbitrary limitation. We are also called to exercise dominion in our leisure time.

Dominion over creation involves both reverencing and protecting the natural creation. We exercise dominion over nature when we admire a sunset or go for a hike in the woods. We do so when we simply let nature be what it is instead of turning it to our own acquisitive uses.

In addition to valuing God's creation in this way, we exercise dominion over it by protecting it from destruction. The advent of the machine as an ingredient in leisure frequently undermines the human race's dominion over the world as God intended it and in many cases ends up destroying the very materials provided for our enjoyment. Quiet lakes are now overrun with gas-guzzling, noisy motor boats that use up the world's nonreplaceable fuel and erode the shoreline. We drive our cars endlessly, polluting the environment, upsetting the ecosystem, and destroying the beauty of nature with roads and parking lots. We turn walkways into motorbike paths until erosion sets in.

A third type of stewardship we can exercise in leisure is stewardship of beauty. Beauty includes both natural beauty and the beauty we find in culture and the arts. A duty attaches to every capacity we possess, including our God-given capacity for beauty. The purpose of beauty in human life is simply enjoyment and pleasure, both for their own sake and the glory of God.

The way to exercise stewardship of beauty is to enjoy it as a gift from God and to resist the utilitarian impulse to despise beauty as an extraneous luxury in life. That impulse is always on the horizon in a culture oriented toward what is useful. The case of Charles Darwin is particularly instructive. In his *Recollections*, written for his children, Darwin recalled that up to the age of thirty, music, painting, and poetry gave him "intense pleasure" and "very great delight."[12] But immersion in science destroyed his aesthetic sense. Darwin reached the point where he could not "endure to read a line of poetry" and where he "almost lost [his] taste for pictures or music." Darwin lamented that "my mind seems to have become a kind of machine for grinding general laws out of large collections of facts," while his "higher aesthetic tastes" atrophied. His final conclusion is instructive:

> If I had to live my life again, I would have made a rule to read some poetry and listen to some music at least once every week; for perhaps the parts of my brain now atrophied would thus have been kept active through use. The loss of these tastes is a loss of happiness, and . . . injurious . . . to the moral character, by enfeebling the emotional part of our nature.

If God did not consider beauty important, he would not have put it into his world and the capacity for its enjoyment into his human creatures.

In leisure we also exercise stewardship (or lack of it) over our bodies and emotions. Here too I would appeal to the kind of person God created each of us to be. He created us physical and emotional creatures. To be good stewards of our bodies and emotions means to maintain their health. There is both a positive and negative side to such health.

Positively, we can use our leisure to foster physical and

emotional well-being. Taking time for leisure is the starting point. The kind of physical activity that is best for us depends on what our daily work is like. For those involved in active physical labor, active recreation is not necessary, though some may choose it for its intrinsic pleasures. Others who sit behind a desk all day need physical exercise to maintain a healthy body.

Much the same pattern prevails in our emotional needs. Most of us need some type of repose in our leisure in order to balance the emotional strain of daily living. But there are also people and occasions where what is most needed is emotional stimulation.

The criterion of physical and emotional health also sets boundaries for legitimate leisure pursuits. Some physical recreations simply have a bad track record for injuries. Boxing, professional wrestling, football, and perhaps skiing fall into this category. Devotees of such sports will not like my negative comments, but the relative likelihood of injury in such sports is a moral issue. Of course many other recreations produce injuries when they are.pursued too aggressively and in an overly competitive way. There is no totally safe physical sport. Still, avoiding physical harm in what we choose as recreation and in how we pursue it remains a moral issue.

The criterion of emotional well-being should also influence our choice of leisure activities. The sheer strain of getting to a leisure activity can make it self-defeating. We should also avoid extending our nonleisure problems into our leisure life. In most cases, someone suffering from family discord will not benefit emotionally from watching a movie or television drama dealing with family problems. A salesperson whose life is hemmed with competitiveness is unlikely to be emotionally soothed by a competitive leisure activity. The therapeutic value of leisure lies partly in its being an escape from everyday life.

Yet another type of stewardship that we can exercise in our leisure life is stewardship of the mind and imagination. God did not give us minds and imaginations in the hope that we will spend our leisure in mindless and unimaginative activities. Here, in fact, is a large part of the Christian case against mass leisure, which tends to be mindless and intellectually impoverished.

To develop ourselves intellectually is not necessarily to turn leisure into something utilitarian. It all depends on how we approach it. When we learn because we want to and because it gives us pleasure, our learning is a leisure pursuit. Once we leave school, the quality of our intellectual life depends largely on what we do in our leisure time. The intellectual decline evident in our culture in recent decades is in large measure due to the loss of reading as a leisure activity.

When I speak of stewardship of the imagination, I have in mind especially the arts. They too have fallen upon hard times in a sports-oriented society. Schools struggle to maintain their music program as students inundate the athletic program. To be well-rounded people in God's world means finding time in leisure for art, music, and literature as well as sports.

Stewardship as Concern for the Quality of Our Leisure

Underlying all the types of stewardship we have discussed is a concern for the quality of our leisure life. If excellence in work is a moral virtue, so is excellence in leisure. Here, too, God wants us to be all we can. God created us as multifaceted people with a range of capacities. Leisure presents us with an immense range of opportunities. We obviously cannot participate in every available leisure activity, but we can insure that we are complete people.

As noted previously, one theory of leisure is that it is the place in life where we are free to seek our ideal identity. Freed from the constraints that determine much of our daily lives, in leisure we can more fully choose to become what we aspire toward. It is a moral virtue to aspire toward the best rather than the mediocre.

To do so is to resist the common pattern of our society. One of the foremost authorities on leisure, Sebastian de Grazia, has rightly observed that leisure is not simply free time but "a state of being . . . which few desire and fewer achieve."[13]

Commitment to excellence in leisure means to aspire to be among those who achieve the ideal of enlightened leisure. To do so has virtually nothing to do with our level of income. It has everything to do with our attitude. Laziness in exerting ourselves toward excellence is the greatest obstacle.

Excellence in leisure also depends on our education. This includes but is not limited to the education we receive in schools. One of the best tests of whether people are generously educated is what they do in their leisure time. One of the foremost obligations of education is to educate people for leisure, not simply in the sense of introducing them to recreational opportunities but in fostering well-rounded people who can enjoy excellence in a wide range of cultural activities.

But all education is ultimately self-education. We are responsible for the quality of our leisure life regardless of the nature of our formal education. It is possible to learn how to have a rich cultural and recreational life on one's own initiative. Simply exposing oneself to excellence in these areas develops the capacity for them. Furthermore, no one can rest on what he or she has learned in school because our leisure patterns keep changing throughout the life cycle.

The quest for excellence in leisure extends also to the church. Here too it is glorifying to God when we achieve excellence. If leisure is God's gift to the human race, we should foster an appetite for the best in leisure in the church. Nor would I exempt the church from the educational aspect of leisure. It would be highly desirable if people developed an interest in some excellent leisure pursuit under the auspices of the church.

MODERATION AND BALANCE IN LEISURE

Two of the time honored moral guidelines of the human race are moderation and balance. Their application to a Christian view of leisure is obvious.

Moderation in leisure means steering a middle course between too much and too little. These are of course relative, and there is no objective measurement by which to tell whether we have met the criteria. They vary with our situation and age. But some broad principles will prove helpful.

One measure of whether we are getting enough leisure is the degree to which the purposes of leisure are adequately achieved in our lives. Those purposes (discussed in the opening chapter) include providing a break from work and obligation, relaxation, entertainment, celebration, self-fulfillment, and the nurturing of family and social bonds. If we are notably deficient in these things, we obviously need either more or different leisure.

On the other side of the ledger, there are several tests of whether we are excessive in our leisure. The chief test is whether our leisure renders us incapable of meeting our moral and Christian obligations. These obligations involve time, money, and work. Our obligations in these areas reach out to embrace our devotional life, our willingness to help in church work, our meeting of family responsibilities, and our availability to help people in need.

As earlier parts of this book have shown, these obligations cannot absorb all of our life. When they do, we collapse physically and emotionally. Yet the sense of duty that lies at the heart of Christian morality means that a major portion of our lives is taken up with them. My own reflection suggests that the time we spend on leisure should not exceed the time we spend in service to family, acquaintances, church, and community. In other words, there should be a balance between the nonworking time that we spend on ourselves and the time spent on others.

Moderation in leisure also means avoiding idolatry in leisure. Many people in our society value their leisure (broadly defined to include things they buy for their enjoyment) above everything else. Of special mention is the status of sports as a folk religion in the contemporary world.[14] This is to say that it has the qualities and loyalties that characterize a religion. These include embodiment of a set of values and beliefs held by a culture, the presence of collective cult observances, and a history that is passed on from generation to generation. To these I would add hero worship, intensity of devotion, ability to elicit financial commitment and sacrifice, dominating people's Sundays, and becoming the central life interest of people.

Of course other leisure pursuits are just as capable of becoming a religion. Whenever people do not put God in the center of their lives, they put another interest there. Many of these interests fall into the category of leisure. We can find devotees of cars, culture, physical fitness, clothes, physical appearance, eating, and shopping. By Christian standards, a leisure pursuit has become an idol whenever it absorbs the time, devotion, and financial commitment that God requires of those who follow him.

In addition to moderation, the principle of balance can help us in our leisure choices. One element of balance is that between solitary and social leisure pursuits. Both are necessary ingredients in a full leisure life. Our social leisure, moreover, should include family, friends, and church.

We can also achieve balance among the broad categories of leisure activities. These extend in three general directions. One is sports, games, and recreation, where the emphasis is often on the physical or competitive. A second is culture, where the emphasis is on the mind and imagination. A third is festivity, celebration, and ritual, such as commemorating a holiday or celebrating a birthday. A full leisure life embraces all three categories.

SUMMARY

What we do in our leisure turns out to be a variation on the most basic of all moral issues—the quest for the good life. From a Christian perspective, that quest is a noble one. God wants people to live a life that is good in every way.

A good leisure life meets several moral standards. It contributes to one's personal well-being in constructive ways by opening up possibilities not present in the routine of work and obligation. It also fosters one's relationships to people and God. In all these spheres, leisure is a form of stewardship in which we are called to make the most of what God has given us. Moderation in the amount of leisure we pursue and balance among the types of leisure are also worthy goals.

To achieve high quality in our leisure requires us to choose the excellent rather than the inferior. The goals and moral criteria for our leisure choices can be stated in the words of a famous New Testament passage:

> Whatever is true, whatever is honorable, whatever is just, whatever is pure, whatever is lovely, whatever is gracious, if there is any excellence, if there is anything worthy of praise, think about these things (Philippians 4:8).

To paraphrase the final command, pursue these qualities in your leisure life.

FURTHER READING

Rudolph F. Norden, *The Christian Encounters the New Leisure* (1965).
Harold D. Lehman, *In Praise of Leisure* (1974).
Arthur F. Holmes, *Contours of a World View*, chapter 15 (1983).
Robert K. Johnston, *The Christian at Play* (1983).

Chapter 8, Notes

1. Frank Gaebelein, *The Christian, the Arts, and Truth*, ed. D. Bruce Lockerbie (Portland, Ore.: Multnomah Press, 1985), 228.

2. Harold D. Lehman, *In Praise of Leisure* (Scottdale, Penn.: Herald Press, 1974), 147.

3. C. S. Lewis, *Christian Reflections* (Grand Rapids, Mich.: Wm. B. Eerdmans Publishing Co., 1967), 33-34.

4. Walter Kerr, *The Decline of Pleasure* (New York: Simon and Schuster, 1962), 241.

5. Gordon Dahl, *Work, Play, and Worship in a Leisure-Oriented Society* (Minneapolis: Augsburg Publishing House, 1972), 98.

6. Wayne E. Oates, *Your Right to Rest* (Philadelphia: Westminster Press, 1984).

7. Muriel Dobbin, "Is the Daily Grind Wearing You Down?" *U.S. News and World Report*, 24 March 1986, 76.

8. Oates, 25.

9. Robert Lee, *Religion and Leisure in America* (Nashville: Abingdon Press, 1964), 199-263.

10. Lee, 260.

11. Blaise Pascal, *Pensées*, II, 139.

12. I have taken my quotations from Darwin's *Recollections* from Kerr, 67-68.

13. Sebastian de Grazia, *Of Time, Work, and Leisure* (New York: The Twentieth Century Fund, 1962), 8.

14. The case has been stated at greatest length by Wheaton College professor James A. Mathisen in an as yet unpublished address, "From Civil Religion to Folk Religion: The Case of American Sport," delivered to the Society for the Scientific Study of Religion, Washington, D. C., November 1986.

Conclusion

Work, Leisure, and Christian Living

*M*y concluding remarks are of the integrative, putting-it-all-together type. We will be integrating three things: work and leisure in relation to each other, work and leisure in relation to the Christian doctrines they share, and work and leisure in relation to the contemporary problems noted in the second chapter. The purpose of the first two items is to show how interrelated work and leisure are. The goal of the concluding item is to show that the Christian faith answers the problems posed by work and leisure in the modern world.

WORK AND LEISURE IN RELATION TO EACH OTHER

We often think of work and leisure as being separate from each other. After all, we experience them separately. They serve such different purposes in our lives that it is easy to think of them as opposites.

But work and leisure belong together. Together they make up our daily lives. They are complementary parts of the single whole of our existence. Because this is so, our well-being depends on our satisfaction in both. A leading sociologist of leisure has said that "research in the various social sciences shows that both work and leisure are necessary to a healthy life and healthy society."[1] In his Christian analysis of the same situation, Robert K. Johnston notes that "play and work go together. . . . Christians are created and called to consecrate both their work and their play."[2]

Work and leisure take their meaning from each other. Without leisure, work narrows life down and damages the worker. But leisure by itself also robs a person of fullness. Without work, people feel useless and lack sufficient purpose in life.

Work-Leisure Relationships

How then should we view the relationship between these two necessary ingredients of life? Authorities on the subject have come up with a widely accepted framework of three possible models to describe how work and leisure mingle in people's lives.[3]

One possibility is variously known as the *spillover* or *identity* or *extension* model of leisure. This means that people find their work so satisfying that they carry over their work experiences and attitudes into their leisure. In fact, they may do many of the same things in leisure that they do in work because this is what gives them enjoyment. People in this position do not make a sharp distinction between work and leisure, usually because they enjoy their work and experience a quality of leisure in work.

The second model of how work and leisure combine in daily living is the *compensatory* or *opposition* model. Here people perceive their work and leisure to form a distinct contrast. Leisure serves the function of compensating for deprivations in work, which in this model is ordinarily unfulfilling in one way or another. People in this category deliberately seek out activities that are different from the daily grind because they need a break.

The third way of relating work and leisure is *separation* or *neutrality*. Here people keep their work and leisure in separate compartments. In the words of Parker, "the neutrality pattern consists of having leisure activities which are generally different from work but not deliberately so, and of appreciating the difference between work and leisure without always defining the one as the absence of the other."[4]

Is one of these models more Christian than the others? Robert Johnston thinks so.[5] He rejects the identity model that extends work into leisure and the "split" model that values leisure as a compensation for what is lacking in work. Johnston prefers the model that assigns separate value to work and leisure. But work and leisure are more interrelated than this view allows.

We need to be slow to baptize any one of the three models as being more Christian than the others. Before we weigh the merits of the individual models, we need to note the broad principles that underlie any Christian view of the relationship between work and leisure. Once we have done so we will find that these principles might be practiced within all three of the models.

We should also note that some writers use the term "integrated" in misleading ways when discussing the relationship between work and leisure. To the extent the three models regard work and leisure as complementary parts of a whole, all three are equally integrated. The question is how to integrate these complementary activities.

The foundational principle is that both work and leisure are good. God created both of them for the benefit of the human race. This means we must reject one of the commonest tendencies of the human race through the centuries—the tendency to regard either work or leisure as good and the other as bad. My guess is that most people in our culture subconsciously regard leisure as good and work as bad. The opposite viewpoint occurs whenever an overly strong utilitarian ethic makes people feel guilty about leisure.

The wisdom of social science research tells us that people function best when their attitudes toward work and leisure are integrated—when both are valid as complementary parts of a whole. Parker writes, "Maximum human development in both work and leisure spheres requires that they be complementary and integrated rather than that one be regarded as 'good' and the other as 'bad.'"[6]

Christian theology says the same thing. According to Genesis 2, the Bible's story of life in Paradise, people in a state of perfection performed the work of cultivating the garden. But they also enjoyed the beauty of the garden, human companionship, and the worship of God.

The complementary nature of work and leisure is reinforced by the fourth commandment, which states:

> Six days you shall labor, and do all your work; but the seventh day is a sabbath to the LORD your God; in it you shall not do any work . . . for in six days the LORD made heaven and earth, the sea, and all that is in them, and rested the seventh day (Exodus 20:9-11).

Here we find the God-ordained pattern of work and rest in complementary rhythm.

With this as the framework, all three of the models for relating work and leisure can be Christian. Everything depends on the specific situation of a given person. There are pluses and minuses in each model, and we need to be aware of these.

For example, people whose work tends to be inherently fulfilling enjoy a very great blessing. People whose work possesses the leisure qualities of freedom, self-fulfillment, and enjoyment already have leisure in their lives before they leave their work at the end of the day. It is natural that such people would experience a lot of continuity between work and leisure. Nor is the autonomy of play necessarily threatened in such continuity. Leisure in work is still leisure.

But there is a price tag attached when people's avocation (what they most enjoy doing) is also their vocation (what they do for a living). One of the functions of leisure stressed throughout this book is its status as a break from routine and obligation. This is what gets lost when people work in their free time.

The Christian view that we need times of rest from work, and have a moral obligation to spend time with family and friends, sets a limit to the practice of merging work and leisure. The biblical sabbath leaves no doubt about the need to include breaks between work and rest in our lives.

When we consider the second model, which stresses the contrast between work and leisure, we again need to be balanced in our assessment. It is a law of human nature that we need retreats from burdensome reality. When work is tiring or unfulfilling, there is nothing wrong with seeking compensation in leisure. I suspect that people who fall into this category often value leisure more than the person whose work is of the type that encourages work "after hours." Paradoxical as it may seem, I sometimes find the prospect of an evening at home more inviting when I know I am too tired to do more work after dinner.

But of course there are problems here, too. People whose work has qualities of leisure in it probably have more overall leisure in their lives. Furthermore, several studies have found that leisure does not, in fact, compensate for lack of satisfaction in the workplace.[7]

A similar ambivalence occurs when we weigh the pattern in which work and leisure are largely independent of each other in a person's life. On the positive side, this model is capable of protecting the separate integrity of both work and leisure. Both can be valued for what they are in themselves, without having to answer to the other. In this they respect the boundaries God has established between the spheres of work and leisure.

But here, too, there can be problems. We function best when we are whole people. Our work is impoverished if our play never extends to our fellow workers, for example. We become split personalities when we live in two different worlds having no significant carry-overs. In the fourth commandment, the worker does not cease to be the same person when he or she rests from work. Later in this chapter I will note the Christian doctrines that apply equally to work and leisure, and here too we will see that we cannot be totally separate people when we work and play.

In sum, we should avoid trying to find *the* Christian model for the relationship between work and leisure. There are too many variables to allow for a single right relationship. That relationship varies with people, type of work, and even day of the week.

In general, the main influence on our leisure patterns is the nature of our work. The less leisure quality we can import into our work, the more separation between work and leisure will be desirable. If our work wears us down physically or emotionally, our leisure will involve a high degree of contrast to our work. But if our work itself contains a balance between solitude and social interaction, between physical exertion and repose, our leisure is likely to resemble our work in these same ways.

The important principle underlying everything is that work and leisure are complementary parts of a God-ordained whole. To maintain the importance of both will help keep either from becoming an idol that usurps all of a person's devotion.

Another aspect of the relationship between work and leisure is that even though the content of the two may be very different, we can strive to import the ideal qualities of one into the other. The usual assumption is that our work will be enriched if we can incorporate the qualities of leisure into it, including a sense of choice in what we are doing, enjoyment, creativity, and self-fulfillment. But the influence can flow in the other direction as well. Our leisure will be richer if it produces some of the same satisfactions that work at its best provides, including a sense of accomplishment, purposefulness, action (as opposed to idleness), and good use of time.

We might profitably recall the diagram on time usage from early in this book. Between the poles of work and leisure is a category of semileisure. It consists of activities that are obligatory but that can assume some of the positive qualities of leisure. Cooking can be routine work shading off into drudgery, but it can also be semileisure if (for example) it involves the creativity of trying a new recipe. One way to redeem work from the curse is to move as much of it as possible into a realm that makes it share the refreshment we associate with leisure.

If I am right in saying that we must avoid christening any one model as the Christian view of the relationship between work and leisure, we are free to see partial truth in some common formulas that by themselves are deficient. There has been a long debate, for example, over whether we work in order to live or live in order to work. Christian writers on the subject (including such a towering figure as Dorothy Sayers) imply that the second is the Christian position. I question this conclusion; it is as incomplete in itself as the other formulation. There is a measure of truth in both statements.

Similarly, people argue about whether we play in order to work or work in order to play. I do not see why we would try to choose between these. Our sense of balance tells us that there is truth in both ideas.

THE SHARED THEOLOGY OF WORK AND LEISURE

Further unity between work and leisure will emerge if we consider the Christian doctrines that apply to them both. In earlier chapters we discussed the theology of work and leisure separately. This is a good time to put them together.

Both work and leisure are rooted in the biblical doctrine of creation. God created both of them. In fact, God himself alternately worked and rested when he created the world. In the Garden of Eden, moreover, he prescribed that people would combine work and leisurely enjoyment. The fourth commandment of the decalogue roots both work and rest in God's creation of the world. We can therefore speak of both work and leisure as creation ordinances.

A second principle that work and leisure share is time. Both occur in time. Together they make up our daily allotment of time. The more time we spend on one, the less time we have for the other. When we realize they are this interrelated, we are in a better position to exercise the balance between them that a Christian outlook encourages.

Work and leisure also share the Christian endorsement of pleasure or enjoyment. Contemporary attitudes would have us believe that we can expect to find enjoyment in leisure, while work is incurably unpleasant. The Bible suggests something different. As intended by God, both work and leisure should be pleasurable. One of the things that makes the book of Ecclesiastes so refreshing is its fusion of work and leisure in a zestful enjoyment of life: "Behold, what I have seen to be good and to be fitting is to eat and drink and find enjoyment in all the toil with which one toils. . ." (Ecclesiastes 5:18).

Another Christian doctrine that applies equally to work and leisure is the doctrine of sin. Human sinfulness makes possible the abuse of work and leisure. Some of the abuses are identical. In both work and leisure we can be guilty of idolatry, of ingratitude, of poor stewardship, of sloth. Both work and leisure can be corrupted by immoral practices and attitudes. We can also make the mistake of undervaluing either work or leisure.

Work and leisure also share a quality of worship in the broad sense of that which makes us conscious of God and relates us to God. In this definition, our work can be an act of worship—something we undertake in obedience to God's call, in dependence on him, and in a spirit of service to him and to humanity. Leisure too can be worshipful. It makes us grateful to God by making us aware of his gifts. It affords moments of reflection when we think about God.

Both work and leisure call for moderation. To pursue one or the other single-mindedly makes us unbalanced. Excessive attention to either leads to a dereliction of the duty we owe to ourselves, our families, and our society. The rule of "neither too much nor too little" applies to both work and leisure.

Finally, the doctrine of stewardship joins work and leisure. God is the giver of both. He holds us responsible for our actions in both spheres. What both work and leisure require from us is a commitment to excellence—a desire to make the most of what God has given, in a spirit of gratitude for what has been given.

To sum up, work and leisure are obviously much closer to each other than we might naturally think. Despite the difference in content between the two in most people's lives, the same Christian doctrines tend to be applicable to them. They are, truly, complementary parts of a single whole.

CHRISTIANITY AND CONTEMPORARY PROBLEMS IN WORK AND LEISURE

This book has been based on a premise that work and leisure need rehabilitation in the modern world and that the Christian faith can contribute to that process. We should, therefore, take another look at the contemporary problems outlined in chapter 2 in light of the Christian principles we have explored in the second half of the book.

Christianity and Contemporary Problems in Work

One problem is an excess of work in what is, after all, a work-oriented society. For some people, at some income levels and at some stages of their life cycle, there are no easy answers. There is simply too much to be done at many points in life.

But when we inquire honestly into the excess of work in the modern world, we find that some of it is avoidable. Much of it is engendered by an acquisitive lifestyle that could be simplified if people chose to do so. Some people work excessively because they worship the success that attends such work, and others because they have not learned to value anything besides work.

The Christian response is to insist that people have been made to rest, play, and worship as well as work. One day in seven is exempt from work. One of its purposes is to protect workers from themselves. The Christian faith sets limits to the impulse to work. It declares a rhythm of work and rest, obligation and freedom.

A second malady that afflicts the worker today is dissatisfaction with work. Nor should we direct all the blame for alienation on the job to a technological age. There were as many unfulfilling jobs before the technological revolution as there have been since. Furthermore, no job is satisfying all of the time. Some tasks, whether around the house or in the workplace, are inherently unpleasant or unfulfilling. What does Christianity say to this problem?

For one thing, it does not deny the problem. It does not share the naive optimism about work that nineteenth-century Romanticists expressed, nor the false posters of beaming workers displayed in Communist countries. Christianity acknowledges an element of curse in work. It thereby saves us from false guilt about burdensome work.

But Christianity also offers solutions to the problem by supplying attitudes that transform how we regard our work. It assures us that God intends us to work. Added to this is the assurance that God calls us to tasks and that to perform them honorably is to obey God. Further, by elevating the concept of serving humanity, Christianity offers a way to transform work that in itself may be distasteful.

The revolutionary aspect of the Christian doctrine of work is that it focuses on the inner attitude of the worker. This contrasts with the Marxist answer to the problems of alienation in work. The Marxist solution pins its hope on institutional change. A changed social structure will somehow make all work inherently satisfying.

Christianity is not opposed to constructive changes in the values by which people live—changes that would have the effect of eliminating some of the demeaning jobs in our society. But Christianity does not share the confidence of Marxism that structural changes can answer the problems posed by work that does not carry inherent satisfaction. Instead it locates the possibility of finding satisfaction in work in the attitude of the worker.

I should note also that the writing on the subject of work continues to display a rather strong Romantic strain. By this I mean an attitude that is nostalgic for a rural past when people lived close to nature. I ran across numerous statements to the effect that when people lived on farms in earlier generations and centuries, they enjoyed more leisure. After all, these people experienced no cleavage between the place of work and the place of play, as people in an urban setting do.

Speaking as someone who grew up on a farm, I must say that the idealized Romantic view of rustic living bears little resemblance to reality. Farm work has more than its share of sheer drudgery. And as for the setting that supposedly integrates work and play, I would simply ask, What play? On the farm one is never free from the setting of work. The moment one looks out the kitchen window one sees the place of work. The Romantic view, like the Marxist view, is entirely too eager for easy answers that would convince us that the problems of work are essentially external and can therefore be solved by changing the externalities of work. Christianity is more inner-oriented than this.

Christianity speaks to two additional aberrations on the current scene. One is the problem of undervaluing work. The results of such undervaluing are poor work and laziness. The Christian doctrines of vocation, stewardship, and commitment to excellence stand as an alternative to the decline of the work ethic in our day. In a Christian view, all legitimate work is honorable and worthy of one's best effort.

In our society work is overvalued as well as undervalued. Christianity is an alternative here as well. Work is not the highest value in life. It should not occupy all our waking time, nor is it meant to be destructive of our relationships to God and others. The workaholic usually worships success and prosperity. In the place of these goals for work, Christianity substitutes the glory of God and service to humanity. Many in our culture take their identity from their work, but in a Christian view our identity comes from being God's people and new creatures in Christ.

Christianity and Contemporary Problems in Leisure

A Christian response to the problems of leisure in our culture begins with a commitment to protect the quality of leisure life. Such an outlook rests on the twin pillars of knowing that God commands leisure for people and wanting to be a good steward of the gift of leisure. In addition to providing this impetus for guarding and fostering the quality of one's leisure, Christianity offers practical solutions to modern problems in leisure.

For one thing, those who acknowledge the Christian view of the necessity of leisure will find time for leisure. The prohibition of work on one day in seven is the starting point. It shows that a boundary must be drawn around human acquisitiveness. If we take this principle seriously, we avoid the syndrome of the harried leisure class who are so busy acquiring goods and doing the things society expects that they experience a time famine. The words of Jesus stand as an effective antidote: "Consider the lilies of the field"; "A person's life does not consist in the abundance of his possessions."

Another problem in our society is low quality in leisure. This is not surprising, since leisure always reflects the values of an individual or society. Christianity calls people to excellence. Its central truth is that it is not enough to leave fallen humanity where it is. Applied to leisure, this means not being content with the level of leisure most people in our culture seek. The Christian life calls us to something better than the triviality, mindlessness, and immorality that characterize much of the leisure scene today.

As is true of work, leisure in our culture is both undervalued and overvalued. To those who cannot value leisure apart from work or who feel guilty about time not spent working, Christianity affirms the necessity and legitimacy of leisure. The Bible endorses rest, festivity, and enjoyment. Christianity protects the value of the nonutilitarian.

Christianity is equally opposed to those who make an idol of leisure. For one thing, Christian belief asserts the necessity and honor of work. This at once disarms those who over-value leisure at the expense of work. Christianity declares that many things in life are worthwhile in addition to leisure. They include work, worship of God, service to people, and commitment to one's family. When these are given their proper place, one does not have time to overemphasize leisure.

WORK, LEISURE, AND THE BALANCED CHRISTIAN LIFE

The main conclusion this book pushes us toward is a deep appreciation for the provision God has made for human life in the rhythm of work and leisure. That rhythm sounds so simple when we encounter it in the creation account of Genesis and in the fourth commandment that it is easy to miss its significance. Yet all the analysis of the problems of work and leisure in society comes back to the keystone of the goodness of both work and leisure in human life.

Not only are work and leisure good in themselves, they also balance each other and help to prevent the problems that either one alone tends to produce. If we value work and leisure properly, we will avoid overvaluing or undervaluing either one.

Every one of us faces choices in work and leisure. It is a rare person who can be said to "have it all together" in this area. Work and leisure are neither more nor less important than such Christian concerns as personal holiness, evangelism, family, and the church. But work and leisure, unlike the other topics, have not received the attention they deserve and require. When I came to write the chapters that placed work and leisure into a Christian context, I was struck by the scarcity of helpful published material. The church in our century cannot be said to have given its best attention to work and leisure.

My goal in writing this book has been more than to encourage correct thinking about work and leisure in Christian perspective. The right ideas are a starting point. The goal is a Christian lifestyle.

At the heart of Christianity is a conviction that we can

change our patterns of life in a Godward direction. We are not doomed to perpetuate wrong attitudes toward work and leisure. Constructive change is always possible. It may be necessary as well. The choice is ours.

Conclusion, Notes

1. Stanley Parker, *Leisure and Work* (London: George Allen and Unwin, 1983), xii.

2. Robert K. Johnston, *The Christian at Play* (Grand Rapids, Mich.: Wm. B. Eerdmans Publishing Co., 1983), 128, 134.

3. A convenient summary of leading models of the work-leisure relationships can be found in James F. Murphy, *Concepts of Leisure*, 2d ed. (Englewood Cliffs, N.J.: Prentice-Hall, 1981), 44-52. The best extended discussion is by Parker, *Leisure and Work*.

4. Parker, 88.

5. Johnston, 128-34.

6. Parker, xii.

7. These studies are summarized by Geoffrey Godbey, *Leisure in Your Life: An Exploration* (Philadelphia: Saunders College, 1980), 111-12.

Subject Index

Beauty, 189-90, 221-22

Calling, 68-69, 96-97, 136-52

Hospitality, 196-97, 216

Leisure
    biblical view of, 182-205, 210-28
    and the church, 13-14, 36-37,
        58-59, 216-18
    contemporary problems in, 50-58,
        242-43
    defined, 19-21, 8-38
    ethics of, 38-39, 207-28
    and the family, 37, 214-15
    history of attitudes toward, 77-84
    Puritan attitudes toward, 100-110
    relation to work, 231-39
    rewards of, 34-38
    theology of, 181-205, 237-39

Play, 30-31, 198-201
Pleasure, 191-94
Protestant ethic 14, 68-71, 87-111,
    125-26, 131
Protestantism 13, 14, 68-69, 81,
    87-111
Puritans
    on leisure, 14, 15, 81, 83-84,
        100-111
    on work, 12, 15, 68-69, 87-100,
        125-26, 134-51, 155, 171-72, 176

Sabbath, 182-85
Semileisure, 20-21
Stewardship, 152-55, 219-25
Sunday observance, 99-100, 218

Television, 31, 54-55
Time, 19-22, 29-31, 50-52, 213,
    220-21

Underemployment, 49
Unemployment, 49

Vocation, 68-69, 96-97, 136-52

Work
    biblical view of, 120-56, 159-77
    and the church, 12-13, 45-46, 58-59
    classical attitude toward, 64-65,
        121-22, 125
    contemporary attitudes toward,
        11-13
    contemporary problems with,
        43-49, 239-41
    defined, 19-28
    ethics of, 27-28, 159-77
    history of attitudes toward, 63-77
    Marxist attitude toward, 72-73
    Protestant attitudes toward, 87-100,
        125, 134-51, 155, 171-72, 176
    relation to leisure, 231-39
    theology of, 119-56, 237-39

Worship, 182-85, 204, 218, 238

247

Scripture Index

Index of Persons